Look to the Rock

Look to the Rock

*The Anglican Papalist Quest
and the Catholic League*

Michael Walsh

CANTERBURY
PRESS
Norwich

© Michael Walsh 2019

First published in 2019 by the Canterbury Press Norwich
Editorial office
3rd Floor, Invicta House
108–114 Golden Lane
London EC1Y 0TG, UK
www.canterburypress.co.uk

Canterbury Press is an imprint of Hymns Ancient & Modern Ltd
(a registered charity)

H
Y
M Ancient
N &Modern
S

Hymns Ancient & Modern® is a registered trademark of
Hymns Ancient & Modern Ltd
13A Hellesdon Park Road, Norwich,
Norfolk NR6 5DR, UK

British Library Cataloguing in Publication data

A catalogue record for this book is available
from the British Library

978 1 78622 058 5

Typeset by Regent Typesetting Ltd
Printed and bound in Great Britain by
CPI Group (UK) Ltd

Contents

Listen to me, you that pursue righteousness, you that seek the Lord. Look to the rock from which you were hewn.

Isaiah 51.1

I tell you, you are Peter, and on this Rock
I will build my church.

Matthew 16.18

List of Figures

A Note from the Author

This book came about through a chance conversation between myself and Mark Woodruff, the current Priest Director of the Catholic League, at a dinner hosted by the Roman Catholic weekly, *The Tablet*. The topic, I have to confess, lay somewhat outside my comfort zone, but the considerable attraction of this particular undertaking was the possibility of having the Catholic League's archives in my study, rather than having to visit some library to consult them. At the end of this exercise, however, I know far more about the Church of England in general, and especially about those who struggled against the odds (and the 'odds' included members of the Church's hierarchy and Parliament itself) to keep alive the Catholic tradition within the Anglican Communion. So much of what the early members of the League fought for has now become commonplace within the C of E, and the League, though not alone in the battle, deserves some considerable credit.

There is one thing I ought to explain. There have been two earlier histories of the League, those by Brian Doolan and Robert Farmer: details are in the bibliography. Both were obviously writing at least in part from personal knowledge, and neither of them gave much of an indication whence came the sources of their information. This made launching out on a new history to mark – somewhat belatedly – the League's centenary, a little difficult. I decided, therefore, that I would footnote everything. There may as a consequence perhaps be rather too many of them for the reader's comfort, but better that, I felt, than none at all. While I am not claiming to have written the definitive version of the League's history, I suspect there may never be another one, but historians of the Church of England itself will have somewhere to look: the League has very rarely figured in the histories of the C of E, which is a pity: it represented and, as I write, continues to represent, a significant strand within Anglicanism.

As I said at the outset, writing about the Catholic League lay outside my comfort zone. I am therefore especially grateful to those who have helped me on the way, particularly David Chapman – again, as I write, the League's General Secretary – Prebendary Brooke Lunn who entertained me so generously in the Charterhouse, and Frs Kevin Eastell and Michael Rear, the past and the present Presidents respectively of the League. Above all, I would like to thank Fr Mark Woodruff, not just for commissioning this book but, through his many emails, educating me in the ways of the Church of England in particular, and in ecumenism in general. The Church of England, thanks to this commission and his advice, no longer lies quite so far out of my comfort zone. Still, I am sure I didn't get everything right. The blame is mine, no one else's.

Michael Walsh
23 February 2019

Foreword

BY BISHOP JOHN HIND

This book explores a significant chapter in the story of attempts since the Reformation to restore ecclesial communion between the Church of England and the See of Rome, both as the church of Peter 'the Rock', and as 'the rock from which we were hewn' in the pleasing pun of its title. Among these attempts have been a number of 'unofficial' initiatives. Although these have frequently been ignored by the 'official' narratives of ecumenical dialogue, they have played an important part not only in motivating individuals and groups towards unity but also in preparing the way for the formal dialogues between separated ecclesial communities, and particularly ARCIC (the Anglican and Roman Catholic International Commission) and IARCCUM (the International Anglican and Roman Catholic Commission on Unity and Mission). The publication of this book is especially timely, given the apparent present retreat from the vision of full visible unity: ecclesial, sacramental communion.

While much has been written about the Malines conversations in the 1920s and the formal dialogue that began with the Malta Report (1968), the full history has still to be written of the unofficial – and usually ignored or disparaged – attempts of those involved in the Catholic League, its predecessors and parallel bodies. Michael Walsh's study helps make up that lack.

The story of the Catholic League is a fascinating supplement to the history of the ecumenical movement and of the Church of England since the early twentieth century. It is a story of hope and disappointment, of unrealistic expectations and at times some unedifying battles – with not a little of the spice of 'naughtiness' on the part of those of its leaders who clearly enjoyed their struggles with the authorities.

Appropriately the book starts with ecclesiology. Less happily, however illuminating, this is 'ecclesiology' in the usual nineteenth-century meaning of the word, referring not to the theological understanding of the Church but to the architecture and furnishing of church buildings, and to the 'choreography' of liturgy. Whether deliberately or not, the author has put his finger on one of the abiding problems of what might for shorthand be described as modern 'Anglo-Catholicism'. Commentators have often drawn attention to the distinction between 'aesthetic' and 'ascetic' Catholicism. Starting where he does, Michael Walsh is soon able to introduce Fr Fynes Clinton, who combined an interest in aesthetic ecclesiology with an equal passion for understanding the universal Church, breathing with both its lungs, East and West. These two tensions, between aesthetics and theology on the one hand and between 'Romanism' and universal Catholicism on the other, help explain the inability of Anglo-Catholics (and even Anglo-Papalists) over the years to speak with a united voice.

Although Michael Walsh understandably concentrates on the Catholic League itself, he does not ignore its antecedents in men like Ambrose Phillips de Lisle and Spencer Jones. To understand what drove their vision of unity, it is necessary to go even further back. The story was fascinatingly told by George Tavard in his classic, *The Quest for Catholicity*, which traces this Anglican 'quest' through successive generations. Tavard began with Thomas Cranmer and Stephen Gardiner, seen as speaking for two strands of the Church of England in the Reformation period, and with the Elizabethan attempt to find a *via media*. Commenting on the lasting legacy of these strands, Aidan Nichols has argued that, as a result of history 'the Church of England is really three churches rolled into one. It is at one and the same time a Church of a classically Protestant stripe, a Church of a recognisably Catholic stripe, and a Church of a Latitudinarian or what would later be called "Liberal" stripe.' It is important to set the Catholic League in the context of this ecclesiastical (even ecclesiological) diversity.

The League and its members were not alone in reading the history of the Church of England in a particular way, frequently incomprehensible to other schools of thought.

For the 'Anglican Papalists', the Anglican tradition began with the mission of Pope St Gregory the Great. Because of his apostolic care in sending St Augustine of Canterbury to do what he could not do himself, the English Church can only be understood in relation to its Roman mother, even though for some centuries this has meant hostility rather than intimacy. England was evangelized from Rome, and historically the unity of the Church in England and the patriarchal jurisdiction of the Archbishop of Canterbury were both dependent on the link with Rome and the Pope's grant of the pallium, as a sign and symbol of the authority that comes from Peter. England as a nation arose from the unity of the English Church, which, whatever distinctive features it may have had, was dependent on the Church of Rome.

For those who read the pre-Reformation history of *Ecclesia Anglicana* in this way, it was natural to judge the English Reformation in a negative way. Nevertheless, despite the rupture there have always been those who believed in and sought a more visible expression of a wider unity. In the turbulent years of the sixteenth century, some saw this unity as with other 'reformed' churches. Ever since the 1530s, however, others have continued to see the Church of England as a detached part of the Western Church and have sought to heal the breach with Rome. During the seventeenth century a notable group of theologians, who have come to be known as 'the Caroline Divines', emphasized both the continuity of the contemporary Church of England with its medieval past and also located it firmly within the *Una Sancta*. This inevitably raised questions about the nature of and requirements for unity – and for the place of the Church of Rome.

These themes re-emerged clearly with the Oxford Movement and its assertion of the spiritual independence and authority of the Church. This inevitably and directly led to an emphasis on the essential character of the Church as instituted and willed by Christ and led by His Spirit. It entailed fresh thinking about the relationship between the separated parts of the Church. Despite hostility, and the weakness exposed by high profile departures for the Roman Catholic Church, the Oxford Movement transformed the face of the Church of England in a remarkably short space of time.

I have already mentioned Michael Walsh's reference to a particular set of Anglican contributions to the quest for unity which are rarely mentioned in the conventional narrative. They are almost, as it were, 'airbrushed' out of the story. These are what might be described as the 'Anglican Papalists'. An early nineteenth-century Anglican convert to the Roman Catholic Church, Ambrose Lisle March Phillipps de Lisle is particularly associated with the Association for Promoting Christian Unity. He was deeply disappointed when, partly as a result of the influence of Cardinal Manning, the Holy Office banned Catholics from participation in the Association. The eccentricity of some other promoters of the Association, such as the Anglican George Frederick Lee, may not have encouraged much enthusiasm in Rome in the Phillipps project. Phillipps was and remains important, however, because of his conviction that, in order to be true to itself and even ultimately to its own formularies, the Church of England must be reconciled to its Roman mother. He ignored, of course, the other strands of post-Reformation English religious tradition, but he was not alone in that. Part of the problem of 'Anglicanism' is precisely that the devotees of each 'strand' tend to claim a monopoly on 'authentic' Anglicanism.

Phillipps may well have been naïve, but he was charitably naïve and lived in the hope that what was dreamable (in Christ) was possible. He thought, as the author of Tract 90 had thought, that, interpreted at their best, the 39 Articles of Religion and the decrees of the Council of Trent were compatible. That such a notion seems as surprising to the popular mind today as it did in the nineteenth century says more about the popular mind than it does about the issues at stake. It also illustrates how unaware many Anglicans and Roman Catholics are of the prehistory of Newman's Tract 90, which rested on a similar seventeenth-century attempt from the pen of Christopher Devenport (*alias* Franciscus Sancta Clara).

Ambrose Phillipps believed that correct understanding of the formularies, the history and the present trajectory of the Church of England would lead inexorably to an overwhelming desire for Catholic unity. Confident in these convictions, he always hoped for corporate rather than individual conversion. Lee's rather weird later history, including his involvement with *episcopi vagantes*, should not blind us to the ground-breaking nature of the Association's vision – nor, for that matter, should Phillipps's curious and indefensible notion of the 'branch theory' of the Church, so beloved of certain Anglo-Catholics.

Another hugely important figure in this story was the American Franciscan, Fr Paul Wattson, who inaugurated the Church Unity Octave in 1908 while he was still an Anglican. It is often forgotten that the original vision for the Octave was explicitly of prayer for the reconciliation of Anglicans with the Holy See. The dates 18 January (the Feast of the Chair of St Peter) and 25 January (The Feast of the Conversion of St Paul) were deliberately chosen with this in mind. It would ultimately be combined with other initiatives to produce the Week of Prayer for Christian Unity as we know it today. Wattson's book, *Prince of the Apostles: A Study* (1907), was based on articles written with his friend, the English priest Spencer Jones (who was also his collaborator in establishing the Octave), for the journal *The Lamp*. The stall is set out uncompromisingly:

> the purpose of the following volume is to present to Anglo-Catholics a careful study of the prerogatives of St Peter, as Prince of the Apostles, and the relation we shall assume to the apostolic see of Rome in order to save the Anglican Communion from a relapse into the same unhappy conditions of unbelief and worldliness which succeeded the Laudian revival and era of the Caroline divines. Unless some new forward impulse can be given to the Catholic revival of the last century, reactions towards this destructive criticism and bald rationalism is inevitable, and this new volume is designed as a contribution to the solution of the grave problem that confronts the Catholic wing of the church at the present hour.

This may be enough to illustrate the antecedents of the Catholic League, providing part of the evidence that the tradition survived Wattson's submission to Rome. Dom Gregory Dix, world-renowned author of *The Shape of the Liturgy*, and Father Hope Patten, restorer of the Shrine of Our Lady of Walsingham in the Church of England, also prove the point. Hope Patten wrote to an American priest friend, 'I am more and more coming to the opinion that Catholics in communion with Canterbury must consider the example of the Wee Frees of the Scots – the day cannot be far off when some of us will have to go out into the desert – and there prove our catholicity – after which perhaps a united body may be formed as a link.'

In the previous century, the Tractarians had appealed to antiquity. In doing so they were not innovating, but simply continuing a long Anglican tradition. Listen to some words of Lancelot Andrewes: 'One canon reduced to writing by God himself, two testaments, three creeds, four general councils, five centuries, and the series of Fathers in that period – the centuries that is, before Constantine, and two after, determine the boundary of our faith.' And, of course, Blessed John Henry Newman: 'I had a supreme confidence in our cause; we were upholding that primitive Christianity which was delivered for all time by the early teachers of the Church, and which was registered and attested in the Anglican formularies and by the Anglican divines.' Nor should one omit the frequent Anglican appeal to the so-called Vincentian Canon – which has been believed everywhere, always and by all (a 'canon' or rule – it is often conveniently forgotten – originally penned to discredit St Augustine's perceived innovations in the doctrine of grace!).

It is, however, all very well, indeed necessary, to refer the Church to its foundations and the first few rows of stones built on them. But what about the living presence of the Spirit in Christ's Church, in the hearts and minds of believers today (as yesterday and tomorrow), inspiring both the *sensus fidei* and the capacity of the Church to teach authoritatively? Without this, there is a danger of making the Church a kind of conservation society. This was, after all, one of the issues at stake between Cranmer and Gardiner. This critical question was raised obliquely by Cardinal Walter Kasper, an undoubted friend of the Anglican tradition, in an address at a meeting of Church of England bishops at Market Bosworth in June 2006, a remarkable lecture which some have said showed more knowledge of Anglican history and ecclesiology than possessed by many of his hearers. Cardinal Kasper spoke particularly of St Cyprian, to whom Anglo-Catholics of all kinds had traditionally appealed. That his address was ridiculed by some says more about his critics than it does about Cardinal Kasper (or even, for that matter, St Cyprian and his notable Anglican apologists).

Catholics, stressing as they do catholicity across the world and across the ages, have to give an account of how 'the faith once delivered to the saints' can be proclaimed in different cultural, social and philosophical environments. The issue of the 'development of doctrine' is always with us. Divisions in Christendom have left separated churches to evolve their own responses. Conflicts, for example, over the Jesuit missions in Asia and South America, and the issues of Anglican 'provincial autonomy', illustrate the Church's constant need to express the changeless gospel in an ever-changing world. *Gaudium et Spes*, Vatican II's Pastoral Constitution on the Church in the Modern World, was a remarkable mid-twentieth-century attempt to articulate a modern answer. It needs, of course, always to be read in conjunction with *Lumen Gentium*, the Council Dogmatic Constitution. Many contemporary debates (and actual or potential divisions) within both the Roman Catholic Church and the Anglican Communion also show, only too clearly, the need for separated Christians to face these questions together.

This may seem far from the subject of this book. But one need only think of the famous address by Bishop Frank Weston to the Anglo-Catholic Congress of 1933 to see how the Catholic instinct leads inexorably to questions of social justice, as well as to the worthy liturgical celebration of the 'mystery of faith'. Michael Walsh tells the story of the struggles Anglo-Catholics had in the late nineteenth and early twentieth centuries to incorporate (or reincorporate) elements of worship from the Roman Catholic Church into their parishes. Church of England bishops demanded the removal of tabernacles and inhibited from ministry priests who gave Benediction of the Blessed Sacrament. Now, however, faculties are given for tabernacles and even diocesan bishops give benediction. A century ago, who could have imagined that in the early twenty-first century Anglican bishops would participate in *ad limina* visits to the tombs of the apostles (to the Church of Peter and Paul)? In 1896 Pope Leo XIII declared orders conferred under the Ordinal of Edward VI 'absolutely null and utterly void'. Yet in 1966 Pope Paul VI placed his own episcopal ring on the finger of Archbishop Michael Ramsey.

Perhaps most remarkable of all, the possibility, and even the necessity, of a universal ministry of unity is now firmly on the ecumenical agenda. Papalists need no persuading of this, seeing the Petrine ministry as a divinely provided protection for local, and especially national or provincial churches, from dominance by their local culture. Not the least of the roles of such a ministry is to safeguard legitimate diversity, so that the local churches, responsive to their own culture, can both be seen as authentic expressions of the *Una Sancta* and make their appropriate contribution to the universal culture of the Catholic Church. The acknowledgement by Pope St Paul VI in an address to the members of the Secretariat for the Unity of Christians in April 1967 that 'The Pope, as we well know, is undoubtedly the greatest obstacle on the path of ecumenism' (not a judgement with which all would concur!), and the imaginative suggestion by Pope St John Paul II in 1995 in *Ut Unum Sint* to 'Church leaders and their theologians to engage with me in a patient and fraternal dialogue on this subject', freed many who had been fearful even to discuss the subject to envisage new possibilities. Of course, since Paul VI and John Paul II much has happened to slow the progress of Anglican–Catholic relations, and even put them into reverse. God, as we know, never wastes anything, however; and in the words of a memorable lecture by Cardinal Cormac Murphy O'Connor in 2009, it remains to be seen whether the achievements of ARCIC up to that point were 'dead in the water or money in the bank'.

Although the Catholic League cannot claim all (or even most of) the credit, many of its aspirations have borne at least partial fruit. When the League was established, weekly communion by lay people was a rarity in both the Roman Catholic Church and the Church of England. In England at least, it is now almost universal. In the early years of the Catholic League, the only authorized eucharistic liturgy in the Church of England was a rite that intentionally broke up the Canon of the Mass, while the Roman Catholic Church only permitted Mass in Latin: the liturgy of both churches is now all but indistinguishable, except to expert liturgists and theologians. Who could have imagined in 1913 that the Roman Catholic Church would have embraced a vernacular liturgy?

In this context, what should we make of Pope Benedict XVI's 2009 apostolic constitution *Anglicanorum Coetibus*, by which, inter alia, he both endorsed previous efforts to reconcile heirs of the English Reformation with the Holy See and also laid down a challenge? The Ordinariates would have made no sense unless the Church of England had been able, even in its separation, to make and form Christians and prepare them for Catholic communion. *Unitatis Redintegratio*, the Decree on Ecumenism of the Second Vatican Council recognized the Anglican Communion as holding a 'special place' among the communions 'in which catholic traditions and institutions continue to subsist' (UR13). Less ink has been spilt in exploring the significance of the word 'subsist' here than in the famous passage in *Lumen Gentium* (LG8) where the 'unique church of Christ' is described as 'subsisting in the catholic church'. In both places, however, the reference is to a substantial reality; and it seems that the Council meant not that Anglican churches have elements that resemble those of the Catholic Church, but that in many cases the inner reality is the same. It is in this context a pity that sometimes 'Anglican patrimony' is understood as almost exclusively a matter of liturgy and certain canonical forms, rather than the totality of the way in which the faithful have been formed. Many of these riches have been shared with the wider Church by individual Anglicans, clergy and laity alike, who have entered the Catholic Church over the decades and have in the process made their own significant ecumenical contribution.

Anglicanorum Coetibus is also a challenge, underlining as it does the remaining obstacles to full ecclesial communion, and thus spurring on the Catholic Church and the Anglican Communion to reinvigorate their efforts towards realizing their publicly declared vision of reconciliation and visible, organic communion.

It is important to recognize that the '*Anglicanorum coetibus*' of the title of the Apostolic Constitution are the 'groups of Anglicans' that had approached the Holy See. It is, however, the individual members of those groups who have to will the provision for themselves and be received personally. In other words, this is not a matter of corporate unity between separated ecclesial communities, but a pathway for individuals (even if they make their way in groups). Thus, while *Anglicanorum Coetibus*, with its recognition of the spiritual reality of Anglican ecclesial life and its provision of a corporate structure for some former Anglicans, makes a contribution to the unity of Western Christendom, it in no way realizes the vision of the Malta Report and ARCIC for reconciliation between the Catholic Church and the churches of the Anglican Communion.

As an exclusively 'Western' phenomenon, it also lacks something of the original ecumenical vision of the Catholic League, which appealed 'to the universal consent of East and West for doctrine, discipline and devotion, rejecting no legitimate practice of the Catholic Church'. Given the then Cardinal Ratzinger's assertion, when Prefect of the Congregation for the Doctrine of the Faith, that nothing more should be required of the Orthodox churches in relation to the papacy than what was the shared patrimony of the first millennium, it would be interesting to ask what comparable statement could be made in relation to Anglicans. In short, what is it that Western 'Catholics' and 'Anglicans' hold in common (in communion) and what divides them? How much in what they hold in common, or in what divides them, is of the *esse* of Catholic identity?

Perhaps, as this question is worked through and the principle for which it was founded remains insistent, there are still further chapters to be written in the story of the Catholic League.

John Hind
January 2019

Bishop John Hind served as Bishop of Chichester, 2001–12. He was Chairman of the Church of England Faith and Order Advisory Group, 1991–2010, and of its Faith and Order Commission, 2010–12. He was a member of the Faith and Order Commission of the World Council of Churches, 1998–2014.

Introduction

Two remarkable Anglican bishops retired to Durham in the 1970s. Animated by the Second Vatican Council's fresh understanding of Catholicism, and its vocation to manifest the universal Church reintegrated in unity, they imparted to students there at the time a large vision of the Church of England set in the context of the one wholeness of the Church. Their conviction that each separate church must in conscience face up to the breaches in Christianity and repair them, as a matter of urgency for the sake of the world and the coming kingdom of Christ, was powerful.

John Moorman, former bishop of Ripon, was respected among Catholics as a scholar of St Francis and the Franciscans. Ideally placed to lead the Anglican observers at Vatican II, he became first Anglican Co-Chairman of the Anglican–Roman Catholic International Commission (ARCIC). His vivid recollections of the Council proceedings and the discussions with ecumenical delegates at its edges conveyed to us the expectations for unity that the Council Fathers had impressed upon him. With other objectives emerging within the Church of England, he told us, however, 'We have done everything we can. It is over to you now.' Michael Ramsey had been the hundredth Archbishop of Canterbury. His lifelong presentation of Catholic order not merely as an historically useful means of organizing the Church's work in the world, but as the essential manifestation of the gospel itself, realizing the kingdom of God and showing Christ to the world in his glory, confirmed to us that the reintegration of the Church's unity was more than desirable: it was necessary. Neither was an Anglo-Catholic 'romanizer'; both were devoted servants of their church's purpose in history, culture and religion. Yet the Congregational background in their families brought an Independent's perspective, seeing their Anglican Church not as an end in itself but as a gift from God's providence, contributing a distinctive English religious tradition to the re-composition of the greater whole, at the same time as recognizing that something missing needed to be restored. Reconciliation between Catholics and Anglicans was therefore the journey ahead, and it needed to involve communion with Peter. In whatever form that might take, it was the inevitable object from the first step, not some last piece in the jigsaw. In this way, they were Papalists.

Those who founded the Catholic League in 1913 had the same feeling that churches in separation were less than the sum of the parts. The preceding century had seen hopes for reconciliation dashed. Rome had forbidden Catholics to remain members alongside Anglicans and Orthodox in the Association for the Promotion of the Unity of Christendom, which Mark Chapman recently judged a romantic 'fantasy of reunion'. In 1896, following requests by Anglicans to resolve an old controversy in their favour, Pope Leo XIII rejected the validity of Anglican Orders. Nevertheless, the reattachment of the two provinces of the Church of England to the Western Church in communion with Peter, 'the rock from which you were hewn', still defined to Anglican Papalists the orientation of their Church's identity, the authenticity of its mission and the purpose of its clergy's ministry. Thus in 1901 Spencer Jones delivered his seminal lecture, 'England and the Holy See', setting out the inescapability of corporate reunion. In 1908, with another Anglican Papalist and future Roman Catholic founder of the Friars of the Atonement, Paul Wattson, he inaugurated what we now know as the Week of Prayer for Christian Unity, addressing the reality of Rome and reunion with it from the outset.

Throughout the League's history, its members and others have made the interventions, while official ecumenism could barely exist, that turned out to be foundational to the later ecumenical movement's pursuit not just of conciliatory relations and collaborations in witness and service, but of dialogue towards visible, organic communion. One of Spencer Jones's hearers in 1901 was Lord Halifax, who took part in the Malines Conversations with Cardinal Mercier in the late 1920s. At one session, Dom Lambert Beauduin, mindful of his encounter with Anglican church life during his exile from Belgium as an Army chaplain in the Great War, proposed an 'Anglican Church, united not absorbed'. The League's leaders welcomed to England Beauduin's disciple, Paul Couturier, as he recast the Wattson–Jones Church Unity Octave into the Week of Prayer. Mark Vickers in *Reunion Revisited* has charted the hidden ecumenism of the 1930s conducted with Roman Catholics by Anglican Papalists, including among others, Henry Joy Fynes Clinton, the effective founder of the League. Dom Gregory Dix, internationally famed for his study, *The Shape of the Liturgy*, demonstrated that the Anglican Papalists' observance of the Roman rite in their parishes and monasteries was not civil disobedience, but internalizing within their Anglican Church that which pertained to the faith and order of the universal Church, taking priority over division and prophesying rapprochement. Couturier's similar lesson of spiritual ecumenism, in which separate Christians adopt one another's riches towards profounder sanctification and thus convergence in Christ and his one Church, found its way into Vatican II's Decree on Ecumenism and in St John Paul II's Encyclical on Christian Unity, *Ut Unum Sint*. The mutual exchange of gifts emerging from separation towards the fullness of the whole, while respecting the integrity of each, has inspired the contemporary theory and practice of Receptive Ecumenism, which provides the structure for progress in the third Anglican–Roman Catholic International Commission.

Despite such figures and currents at play over generations, on which in part the official ecumenism between the Catholic Church and the Anglican Communion could later be built, the papalists' contribution, according to Bishop John Hind's telling observation in his Foreword, has effectively been 'airbrushed' out of the history. Yet the underlying principle of a movement that rejected the branch theory of separated churches – with the same root but which might never graft into each other again – and in favour of corporate reconciliation have proven formative. Its early leaders and supporters have variously been described as eccentric and marginal; but the imagining of a reunion of the whole Church of East and West, and within that of 'the Church of England entire', became Rome's own desire and a mainstream objective within Anglicanism too. For this reason, we asked the distinguished Catholic historian, Michael Walsh, to give his appraisal of the League's contribution in this movement across its history of 100 years or more. We are most grateful to him. We also thank Canterbury Press for seeing that there may be value in reading the League's sometimes lonely witness back into the record.

In light of Vatican II's luminous prospect of repair and reintegration, the League has been an unstinting advocate of ARCIC and its application, the Anglican Centre in Rome, the pastoral and evangelistic need for the Church to be one if it is to be true to Christ, and its very feasibility through profession of the Catholic faith if his mission 'that the world may believe' is to be realized. It has been devoted to a daily spirituality of prayer for unity (especially promoting the Week of Prayer), to mutual reparation for the scars from past divisiveness and to pilgrimage where separated Christians may understand and learn from each other, going deeper into the mystery of the Church and finding communion through the one faith it professes.

Once it was a body reserved to those working from within Anglicanism; in modern times it became open to all who share its approach and objects for the 'reintegration of unity' set forward at the Second Vatican Council. Over the years, many members have become Roman Catholics; so the League has become an ecumenical association of those who do not wish for what Blessed John Henry Newman described as 'the parting of friends', but the corporate reconciliation of their churches. Perhaps the foundation of the Ordinariate of Our Lady of Walsingham under the terms of the 2009 Apostolic Constitution *Anglicanorum Coetibus* realizes corporate reunion in a way desired by many Anglican Papalists ever since the mid nineteenth century, and thus marks the League's last chapter. Certainly it is one form of corporate, or at least collective, reunion. But reintegration of the unity of the Catholic Church and the Anglican Communion as a whole realistically remains far off. All the more reason to hold to the pioneering aim of the League: not to settle for separateness as a way to hold on to what is distinctive, but to insist on the visible, organic unity of Christ's body in all the richness of its diverse gifts, for the simple reason that St Paul demanded it, and the Lord himself prayed for it; and this is as much as to say he is bringing it to pass. The League has offered thanks to God every day for being asked to bear witness to the need for unity in Christ's body the Church, and thus to give a convincing account of the hope that lies within us.

Mark Woodruff
12 February 2019

Fr Mark Woodruff is a Roman Catholic priest of the Diocese of Westminster and Priest-Director of the Catholic League.

I

Ecumenical Challenges

In *Foxes Have Holes*, a glossy supplement to the June 2005 issue of the Catholic League's journal, *The Messenger*, Michael Woodgate wrote of his time as rector of the church of St Magnus the Martyr in the City of London. He began with a brief note on its history from the time of the appointment to the church of his predecessor-but-one Fr Henry Joy Fynes Clinton in 1921:[1] 'With the assistance of the ecclesiastical artist Martin Travers, he transformed the church into what has come to be known as 1920s English baroque. Adding two side altars, enlarging the sanctuary, adding a new high altar and setting up shrines, they beautified what had been a typical if austere Wren City church.'[2]

To say of Travers that he was an 'ecclesiastical artist' is something of an understatement. He produced distinguished work in a variety of media, though his particular skill was in the making of stained glass, a topic on which he lectured at the Royal College of Art from 1924, when he was 38 years old, until his death in 1948. But he also excelled at doing just what Fynes Clinton asked of him, 'baroquizing' churches. The baroque was the style that, together with the addition of 'shrines', most successfully – or so many Anglo-Catholics thought – recaptured the Roman, as in Roman Catholic, spirit. In the wish to bring that Roman culture to London, the two men were closely aligned. Travers had used his ability as a draughtsman to illustrate the publications of the Society of Saints Peter and Paul, founded in 1911 to counter the considerable influence of

---

1 Woodgate, *Foxes Have Holes* (The Catholic League, 2005), says 1920.
2 Ibid., pp. 3–4.

the Revd Percy Dearmer, someone who, like Fynes wished to breathe new life into Anglicanism but in his case by reviving the old English rite of Sarum.

Dearmer, who had been ordained priest in 1892, served from 1901 to 1915 as vicar of St Mary's, Primrose Hill in London. He was himself an artist – he was Professor of Ecclesiastical Art at King's College, London from 1919 to 1936 – and gathered around him a coterie of like-minded artistic friends among whom was Travers. As far as his churchmanship was concerned, however, Travers had more in common with Fynes Clinton than with Dearmer. The Roman style went hand in hand with the current Roman liturgy, not with the long-abandoned use of Sarum. Together with a 'radical move from an aesthetic point of view', Woodgate remarks, 'perhaps even more radical was his [Fynes Clinton's] introduction of the Roman liturgy – in Latin. It is not surprising that St Magnus became a centre of what has been called the "Anglo-Papalist" movement.'[3] Rather than the church of St Magnus the Martyr, it might almost be more accurate to say that during his lifetime – he died in 1959 – Henry Joy Fynes Clinton himself was the centre of the Anglo-Papalist movement: his life accounted for almost half a century of the Catholic League.

Fynes, as he was generally known, came from a long line of Church of England clergymen, three of whom served as successive rectors of the parish of Cromwell in Nottinghamshire, a fairly prosperous living in the gift of the dukes of Newcastle who were remote relatives of the Fynes Clinton family.[4] Henry's father, however, moved south. He served as a curate then as rector of the church of Sts Peter and Paul in Blandford Forum, North Dorset, a rather fine building, one of the few Georgian churches outside London and which boasts of a pulpit designed by Sir Christopher Wren. Henry was born in Blandford Forum on 6 May 1875, and lived in the town until, at the age of 16, he

---

3 Ibid., p. 4.

4 He had his armorial bearing displayed in St Magnus. There is a lengthy genealogy in John Salter's biography of Fynes Clinton, *The Anglican Papalist* (London: The Anglo-Catholic History Society, 2012), pp. 10–15. Salter is himself a distant relative of his subject.

was sent to the King's School, Canterbury. He flourished, and won a scholarship to Trinity College, Oxford, where between 1894 and 1898 he studied Literae Humaniores.

Provided he could persuade a sympathetic bishop – he was already a High Church enthusiast – his degree would at the time have sufficed for ordination as a priest of the Church of England. He himself, however, was determined to undertake a course of theological studies, choosing the staunchly Anglo-Catholic Ely Theological College.[5] Before beginning his year of training, however, he went as tutor to the Morosov family in Moscow for a few months, which left him with an abiding interest in non-Western forms of Christianity. In 1906, he founded the Anglican and Eastern Churches Union, which in 1914 merged with the much older Eastern Churches Association to become the Anglican and Eastern Churches Association (AECA). He served as its General Secretary until, in 1920, he became Secretary of the Archbishop of Canterbury's Eastern Churches Committee: the committee members of the AECA seemed remarkably eager that he take up the Archbishop's post when it was offered him. He had a penchant for founding organizations of one sort or another,[6] not all of which survived though the AECA has done so. It lies well outside the scope of this book, but notwithstanding all the controversy over Anglo-Papalism in which he was engaged, it has to be remembered that Fynes's concern for the Churches of the East was a constant and important feature of his life.

Fynes Clinton was ordained deacon in 1901 and as a priest the following year. While in deacon's orders, he served at St John the Evangelist in Upper Norwood, remaining there until 1904 before going to Brighton for two years, then returning to London, to St Stephen's Lewisham, up to 1914. That year he moved to St Michael's Shoreditch until his appointment to St Magnus the Martyr.

---

5 Founded in 1876, closed in 1964.

6 Michael Yelton describes him as 'an inveterate founder of organisations of various sorts' (*Anglican Papalism: An Illustrated History 1900–1960* (London: Canterbury Press, 2008), p. 20).

There was already a strong Anglo-Catholic tradition in the Church of England, ultimately stemming, in its modern form, from the Tractarians: it has been remarked that Fynes studied at Trinity, Oxford, the college of that most prominent of the Tractarians, John Henry Newman. In 1900, while still a deacon, Fynes attended a sermon at St Mathew's, Westminster, arranged by the Association for Promoting the Unity of Christendom and given by Spencer John Jones, rector of Batsford with Moreton-in-Marsh, a living to which Fr Jones, as he liked to be called, had been appointed in 1887 and which he held for over 40 years. The title of the sermon was 'England and the Holy See'. It was a bold move, given that Pope Leo XIII had just (in 1897) declared in the bull *Apostolicae Curae* that Anglican orders were 'absolutely null and utterly void'.[7] After the sermon, Charles Lindley Wood, the second Viscount Halifax, 'came into the vestry and said "Now you must publish that"'.[8] The sermon became a book, published under the same title two years later with an introduction by Lord Halifax,[9] the leading Anglo-Catholic layman and, from 1868 the chairman

---

7 For the machinations behind this document, see *Absolutely Null and Utterly Void: An Account of the Papal Condemnation of Anglican Orders, 1896*, by the American priest-historian, John Jay Hughes (New York: Corpus Books, 1968).

8 Geoffrey Curtis, *Paul Couturier and Unity in Christ* (London: SCM Press, 1964), p. 59. In a tribute to the Revd Spencer Jones, Fr Vincent McNabb OP speaks of him as 'a deep thinker and holy soul combining qualities both of the martyr and the prophet', and as one whose 'manifest yet humble priestliness fitted him for higher rank than the priesthood', but who 'sacrificed such a hope for the sake of truth and of his undying love of the Church of England. The thought and reasoned thesis of his books ... was dominant in creating a movement which after giving us the Malines Conversations, is now giving us greater than these in the mutual talks and joint action of our religious leaders' (*The Pilot* XI, No. 117, May 1943, p. 36), quoted by Curtis, *Paul Couturier*, pp. 194–5.

9 *England and the Holy See: An Essay towards Reunion* (London: Longmans, Green and Co., 1902). There is a puzzle about this book. The British Library catalogue lists two volumes with this title for the same year, one, labelled '2nd edition', of 264 pages, the other, with the introduction by Halifax with 440 pages. The longer book is hardly likely to be the '1st edition' of the shorter one, but no 1st edition is listed.

of the umbrella organization of Anglo-Catholicism, the English Church Union (cf. below, p. 65n37).[10]

Spencer Jones's arguments for the reunion of the Church of England with the Church of Rome were not new. In 1854, for example, Ambrose Phillipps de Lisle, a convert to Roman Catholicism at the age of 16, founded the Association for Promoting the Unity of Christendom (APUC) to encourage the reunion not just of the Church of Rome with that of Canterbury but likewise with the Orthodox Churches. Nicholas Wiseman, the Cardinal Archbishop of Westminster, was not enamoured of APUC, believing that the hope of corporate reunion would discourage those contemplating individual conversion, but he did nothing to prevent Catholics joining: according to Margaret Pawley, at its height in 1862 there were some 8,000 members, of whom 1,000 were Roman Catholics.[11] Wiseman's misgivings, however, were shared by other English bishops, and towards the end of his life Wiseman changed his mind. He and the other members of the hierarchy petitioned Rome. In September 1864, a rescript of the Holy Office addressed to all the English bishops – *Ad omnes episcopi Angliae* – criticized APUC, and without actually forbidding RCs from being members, urged the bishops to do their utmost to discourage them. In a pastoral letter dated the Epiphany 1866, Henry Edward Manning, who had in May 1865 succeeded Wiseman as Archbishop of Westminster, issued a stern warning against Catholic membership of APUC and listed its theological deficiencies.

Despite these apparent condemnations, the Roman Catholic weekly, *The Tablet*, reported of APUC on 17 October 1868:

In the September of 1858 – a year after the formation of the society – 675 members had been enrolled, and the following numbers were added to the lists in the years enumerated

---

10 He took the post, which he held from 1868 to 1919 and again from 1919 until his death in 1934, at the direct request of the theologian Edward Pusey, one of the original Tractarians.

11 Margaret Pawley, 'Lisle, Ambrose Lisle March Phillipps de (1809–1878)', *Oxford Dictionary of National Biography* (Oxford University Press, 2004), available online at http://www.oxforddnb.com/view/article/7457 [accessed 2 May 2016].

below respectively: In 1859, 833 members; in 1860, 1,060; in 1861, 1,007; in 1862, 1,393; in 1863, 1,202; in 1864, 1,340; in 1865, 1,317; in 1866, 1,401; in 1867, 1,647; in September, 1868, 803; making a total of 12,684. The division of these, as given by the Rev. George. F. Lee, D.C.L., who retires from the office of general secretary, is both curious and significant. Of the 12,684 members of the society, 1,881 we are told belong to the Roman Catholic Church in various countries; 685 are Orientals, 92 are attached to such uncertain or miscellaneous communities, whose names the secretary was unwilling to take upon himself to decline, and 10,026 belong to the Church of England and other Churches in communion with the same.

Two years later, however, attitudes had changed. *The Tablet* described a meeting of APUC as 'grotesque', condemning out of hand the 'branch' theory, the argument that the Roman, Anglican and Greek [*sic*] communions are all branches of the same Catholic Church. It was equally scornful of what it saw as the copying of RC ritual by Anglican clergy.[12]

Though its hopes had been dashed, the creation of APUC revealed that there existed a significant number of Anglo-Catholics, clergy and laity, who were working towards reunion with Rome and likewise a number of organizations, some more ephemeral than others, fostering this Anglo-Catholic sentiment. One such was the Guild of the Love of God. Apparently inspired by the Anglican Benedictine community which had been established on Caldey Island in 1906, the Revd A. V. Magee had begun the Guild in 1910. Fynes Clinton joined as a founder member, serving on its committee. It appeared to flourish. A year after its foundation, it could boast of 900 members and even had a remote branch in Nova Scotia. Two years after it had begun, Magee announced a membership of 2,500. In 1911 and 1912, there were celebrations, both social and liturgical, to mark the anniversaries of the Guild's founding; Fynes Clinton played a prominent part. All, however, was not well.

---

12 *The Tablet*, 17 September 1870, p. 10. The paper had just acquired a new owner, the Revd (later Cardinal) Herbert Vaughan.

An editorial in the 7 March 1913 issue of the *Church Times* drew attention to the dissension:

We hope that the unfortunate differences that have arisen in the Guild of the Love of God may not issue in the division of a guild which seemed to have the prospect of much usefulness. But we fear that the intransigent attitude assumed by certain members of the executive towards the Warden and founder does not make the prospect of unity very bright. The Guild was founded with one object in view, the banding together of those who within the English obedience profess the Catholic Faith and are anxious to promote it. It appears that a determined attempt is being made to commit the Guild to definitions and a policy which had no place in the original conception of the Guild, or in its objects and rules. The spirit which animates this movement is perhaps best illustrated by a phrase in a circular of the promoters of the movement, which speaks, with as little accuracy as sense of humour, of 'the driving out from us of our greatest treasure, our Anglican Benedictine community.' The appeal of the Warden to a real Catholicism, not limited to the modern Roman conception of it and to modern Roman definitions, is represented as an indifference to the cause of re-union, and there is a characteristic refusal to recognize existing facts. But if certain members of the executive prefer to regard that only as 'Catholic' which has Roman sanction, then we can only say that they have little knowledge of the real issues, and that in endeavouring to identify the Guild with that small minority of English Catholics who approve even those extravagances of which the best Roman Catholics are heartily ashamed, they are really hindering the cause which they attempt to serve. The re-union of Christendom will be attained only by the insistence upon what is essentially Catholic, not by the recognition of fundamentally un-Catholic, claims, nor by the sedulous imitation of those who regard us only with amused contempt, and who deny to us the possession of Catholic essentials.

The following week, 14 March, there was a response which presaged the foundation of the Catholic League. The editor noted:

We have received the following letter in reply to some comments on the differences now unfortunately prevalent in this Guild which appeared in our columns last week:

Sir,—We should be obliged if, in justice to us, you would be so kind as to give space to the following reply to your statement in last week's issue concerning the Guild of the Love of God.

(1) It is not only certain 'members of the Executive' who find themselves in unfortunate disagreement with the Warden. It is the majority of the Executive Committee, including all the five executive officers and two others, and excepting only the Warden's personal secretary and one elected member.

(2) The Warden is only the co-founder of the Guild. The other co-founder is one of the Committee who disagrees with him as to his interpretation of the original intention of the Guild.

(3) The Committee do not, and have repeatedly said officially that they do not, 'regard that only as "Catholic" which has Roman sanction.' They have also repeatedly refused, by official resolutions, to 'identify the Guild' with sectional 'extravagances.'

(4) The main points of disagreement are

(a) A proved impossibility of working with the Warden in executive matters.

(b) A steady refusal to have the outlook and attitude of the Guild narrowed to an exclusive and negative Anglicanism in place of the plain Catholicism with which it started, and on which we joined it.

(c) The desire to maintain that perfect charity which is 'anti' to no part of the Catholic Church, and does not rejoice in controversy.

(5) We find ourselves in a large majority both in Committee and Council. But we have no desire to deprive the Warden of any satisfaction he may derive from retaining the name and badge of the Guild of the Love of God.

(6) Accordingly a new Society, 'The Catholic League,' is being set on foot by the Committee. Its objects and outlook are the same as those of the published official statements of the Guild of the Love of God, taken in their plain and grammatical sense. It will seek to unite 'all Catholics.' It will naturally appeal first and foremost to Catholics in communion with Canterbury. It will exclude no faithful Catholic who wishes and is able to join it. It appeals, as the Anglican Communion appeals, to the universal consent of East and West for doctrine, discipline and devotion, rejecting no legitimate practice of the Catholic Church.

You will, therefore, see, Sir, that we and our aims have not been correctly represented by the statement in your last issue, and we cannot but regret the publication of any statement regarding differences in the Guild at the present juncture. A very carefully prepared statement, in which the Committee definitely repudiate the attitude attributed to them by you last week, was at that time under consideration by the General Council. The ordinary members of the Guild knew nothing of the dispute until you told them of it. Your action has unfortunately destroyed any hope which we may have had that the Guild might be held together. We are therefore being compelled to ask the majority who agree with us to join us in a new society.

Our reference to Caldey[13] has been singled out as an example of our spirit. It seemed natural that we should refer to Caldey, and be grieved for its loss, in that it was once the pride of the Warden, as it has always been ours, that the Guild of the Love of God was cradled there.

H. R. Rivers Moore (General Secretary)
P. H. Easter (Organizing Secretary)
Maxwell C. P. Black (Foreign Secretary)
A. E. Page (Treasurer)
R. L. Langford James, D.D. (Editor of 'Caritas')

---

13 The majority of the Anglican Benedictine community, established in 1906 on Caldey Island just off Tenby in South Wales had, under their Abbot Aelred Carlyle, just recently converted to Roman Catholicism.

J. B. Lowder Tolhurst (Co-founder of G.L.G. and first
General Secretary)

H. J. Fynes Clinton (Member of Committee).

Apart from the remark about the difficulty the committee
members found with working with the Warden of the Guild,
A. V. Magee, the letter is short on specifics. Subsequent correspondence, also in the *Church Times*,[14] revealed that there had
been an attempt by Magee to change the rules of the Guild,
seemingly to make it less 'Roman' Catholic. A particular complaint was the removal of explicit reference to the invocation of
the saints, while another, apparently, was the downplaying of
the figure of the Pope. As the letter just quoted had surmised,
the Guild of the Love of God continued its Catholic course, but
now without the Anglo-Papalists.

The Catholic League was inaugurated at a meeting held at
the Holborn Restaurant on 3 July 1913. From the Guild, it
inherited an already functioning committee, headed by Langford James and Fynes Clinton, which set about drawing up a
constitution representing their churchmanship. The objects of
the association were printed in a supplement to the December
1913 issue of *The Messenger*, the League's swiftly established
periodical.[15] 'We desire', it said, 'to promote brotherhood and
union among Catholics, to deepen their spiritual life, and to
encourage the spread of the Catholic Religion.' There was laid
out an elaborate structure of branches, based in churches, each
branch being practically self-governing and independent. The
'working unit' in any branch was the chapter, the chapters being
grouped into provinces and divided into wards. The secretaries
of wards, chapters and provinces were to be lay people who had
been elected to the posts, whereas officers who were clergy were
to be appointed by an elected Superior. The chapters, members

---

14 Cf. issue for 5 September 1913.

15 The appearance of *The Messenger* was, at times, rather irregular, and
the early issues did not have numbered pages. In the references to this publication which follow, therefore, only the month and year will be given.
As it rarely consisted of more than a few pages it should not be difficult to
identify quotations.

were instructed, were to be named after some sacred mystery, while the wards were to have the names of saints.

The committee elected Langford James as the first Superior, and he appointed Fynes Clinton as his Assistant General and Rivers Moore as the General Secretary of the Catholic League. Langford James had not been the first choice. The invitation had originally been made to the Revd Arnold Pinchard of St Jude's, Hill Street, Birmingham, but 'after careful consideration and enquiry' he had decided not to accept.[16] According to *The Messenger,* however, he had first accepted and then withdrawn. In his letter turning down the post, he said that he had thought that the League would be 'a bulwark against Roman aggression on the one hand and Protestant errors on the other'. In this, he added, he had been mistaken. To the *Church Times* he was a little more explicit: 'the vicar of St. Jude's states that he is quite convinced that he should find himself in an equivocal position of great difficulty within the League were he to accept the post, and is sure that he should not prove acceptable in the office to many of the most prominent of its members'.[17] Though he does not say so, Pinchard's decision must surely have been influenced by the adverse reaction to the League's inauguration service held at the parish church of Corringham in Essex.

The proposal for the service came from Clifton Kelway, a licensed lay reader at Corringham and one of the founder members of the Catholic League. The parish was celebrating its patronal feast on Saturday 5 July, and Kelway suggested that the League might join in. An order of service was drawn up and printed. Members were to assemble then make their way in procession to the church singing the Litany of Our Lady followed by the *Salve Regina.* Some accounts suggest that these were sung in Latin, but the service leaflet does not indicate that they were in anything other than English. At the shrine of Our Lady in the church there were prayers, a hymn, then an act of dedication: 'We do hereby place the Catholic League under the Protection and patronage of the most Glorious and Blessed

---

16 *Church Times*, 3 October 1913.
17 Ibid.

Ever-Virgin Mary, the Mother of God, Our Lady of Victory; and of St Joseph her Spouse and the Guardian of the Divine Childhood; and of St Nicholas the Wonderworker, Bishop and Confessor ...' Badges were blessed, members were formally admitted and blessed, as was the 'standard' – presumably the League's banner – and after everyone had recited the League's prayer, a collection was taken 'for the League and printing expenses'.

Unfortunately for the League, the proceedings had been witnessed by John Alfred Kensit, son of the founder of the Protestant Truth Society and by this time its secretary. Kensit, like his father, is regularly described as a 'Protestant agitator',[18] but in a letter circulated by Langford James (and signed also by Fynes Clinton) to members of the League, Langford James simply calls him 'a Protestant spy'. Kensit sent a report of the service to the Bishop of St Albans, Edgar Jacob, who reacted angrily. He banned both Langford James and Fynes Clinton from officiating in his diocese – neither of them were, of course, under the jurisdiction of the Bishop of St Albans – and without consulting him immediately withdrew Kelway's licence as a lay reader.[19] The bishop's ire extended to the rector of Corringham for allowing the service, and he was required to remove a statue of Our Lady from the church. In his letter to the League, Langford James admits he did not send the order of service to the rector, but pointed out that he was known to be in sympathy with the League's aims and that he had himself been asked by the rector to preach at Vespers.[20]

The Bishop of London, Arthur Winnington-Ingram, was more sympathetic, but warned Langford James that, if Bishop Jacob carried out his threat to sue him before the Court of Arches, he could not protect him unless he withdrew from the League: the same held true for Fynes Clinton under the jurisdiction of

---

18 By Michael Yelton, for example, in *Anglican Papalism*, p. 48.

19 The parishioners of Corringham shortly afterwards presented Kelway with a testimonial in thanks for the work he had done in the parish over the previous seven years.

20 A copy of this circular is to be found in the League's archives. It is dated 20 August.

the Bishop of Southwark. The question of defending himself before the Court of Arches, Langford James explained, did not arise. First of all, after consulting the English Church Union, he was of the view that no one in the Catholic tradition could accept the authority of the court, but secondly, perhaps a more important point, church practice was at stake. As he explained in a letter published in the *Church Times* on 15 August, 'The head and front of our offending at Corringham was that our service contained invocations of certain saints. I was threatened with prosecution in the Court of Arches unless I consented to withdraw from the Catholic League. After taking the opinion of several in a position to give adequate advice, I came to the conclusion that it would be unwise to risk the chance of a "legal" pronouncement against Invocation. Therefore, for the sake of the Church, I accepted the terms.'

Langford James resigned as the Superior and both he and Fynes Clinton temporarily withdrew from the League. The new Superior was the Revd E. S. Maltby, the priest-in-charge of St Mary's, South Bermondsey, a mission which he had himself initiated. Maltby was the next object of Kensit's attention. On 2 September he reported to the Bishop of Southwark about a 'service in connection with the now notorious "Catholic League"'. Under the heading of 'Glaring Romanism', he listed the following as having taken place in St Mary's on 21 August:

Rosary of our Lady
Congregational use of Holy Beads
Procession with Mary Image
Litany of Our Lady
Avowal of the Immaculate Conception
Procession of the Host
Benediction and Exposition of the Sacrament
Intercessions to the Host
Worship of the sacred Heart
Collects, Hymns, and Responses in Latin.[21]

---

21 The full report to the Bishop of Southwark constitutes Appendix A in Robert Farmer's *The Catholic League 1913–1988* (The Catholic League, 1989[?]), pp. 17–21.

There was much more to Kensit's report, but the bishop seems to have taken little notice. Such complaints, however, were indicative of the battles which in this period of its existence the League had to fight.

Not that all bishops were hostile. There was much excitement in Catholic League ranks at the expected presence of Frank Weston, a member of the Society of the Holy Cross and, since 1908, Bishop of Zanzibar, at a gathering at St Michael's, Bingfield Street[22] in Islington, North London held on 25 April 1914. 'All members are urged to be present', editorialized *The Messenger*, 'to show him how appreciative we are of the stand he is making for the Faith and Discipline of the Church.'[23] But support from bishops was rare. A memorial, with nearly 8,000 signatures, had been sent to Randall Davidson, the Archbishop of Canterbury, but with no response. 'It is bitter to realise, but one can expect little encouragement in prayer and worship from our Father in God.'[24] On 11 June 1915, according to the Roman Catholic calendar the feast of the Sacred Heart, at St Cuthbert's, Philbeach Gardens, the Apostleship of Prayer was established within the League. It was modelled on the Jesuit-fostered society whose members undertook to pray for certain 'intentions' which changed month by month.[25] In 1916, after the Bishop of Chelmsford, John Watts Ditchfield, threatened to withdraw the licence of the parish priest of St Oswald's,

22 The church closed in the early 1970s.

23 The reference is to the 'Kikuyu' controversy: at a conference at Kikuyu in what is now Kenya in June 1913, Weston had taken a stand against more evangelical bishops from neighbouring dioceses who had shared communion with Congregationalists and Presbyterians, and had proposed an exchange of pulpits.

24 *The Messenger*, March/June 1914.

25 They also committed themselves to a morning offering to the Sacred Heart, a daily decade of the rosary and weekly 'communion of Reparation'. Associated with the Apostleship of Prayer was the 'Tabernacle Treasury', a fund to provide money for monstrances for churches too poor to purchase for themselves this means of displaying and worshipping the Blessed Sacrament. Cf. Brian Doolan, *The First Fifty Years* (Printed for the League by the Crux Press, 1966[?]), p. 12. Other organizations embraced by the League included The Guard of Honour of the Blessed Sacrament, the Women's Retreat Association and the Community of Canonesses Regular of Our Lady of Victory 'following the Order of the Holy Sepulchre' (*The Messenger*, July 1918).

Walthamstow, the intention for members of the Apostleship was 'That the Church of England may be delivered from the State appointment of Bishops and dignitaries'.[26]

At the onset of war in 1914, the League showed itself as patriotic as its fellow countrymen: 'the war must be the first consideration at the present time. The first duty of the men of the League who are able is, therefore, to fight under the banner of St George to slay that vile dragon of German "culture" which we have loathed so long. Let there be no mistake about this. Religious society as we are, our duty of prayer comes second now, and that we pray must not be made an excuse for shirking work.'[27] The downplaying of prayer was surprising – and soon rectified. *The Messenger* for June/September 1915 reported that yet another society had been established within the League, 'the Living Crown of Our Lady of Victory', its members undertaking to say daily a decade of the rosary under the general intention 'that Catholic soldiers may not be deprived of the sacraments by the unfaithfulness or ignorance of Ministers and Authorities of the Church'. The following year, the General Secretary noted 'Those who were able to be present at the Requiem Mass at St Michael's, North Kensington, must have felt how real a part the League is playing in the great struggle which, in spite of the confusion of issues which appears on the surface, is in essence the fight for the faith of Christ and His Church which can be traced back to the revolt from that Church and the repudiation of the religion of Mary and Her Child.'[28] (It was further noted that scapular medals – at a cost of a shilling each – were to be sent to every member of the League serving in the armed forces.)

The problem was prayers for the dead, at the very least a controversial issue within the Church of England. After complaints from some of the Church's more Protestant members, the Bishop of London had felt himself obliged to prohibit requiem Masses in his diocese.

The war, despite all the suffering, had its compensations, at least in the view of Rivers Moore, the General Secretary.

26 *The Messenger*, January/March 1916.

27 Ibid., September/December 1914.

28 Ibid., January/March 1916.

Victory over Prussia, he believed, was the opportunity for 'the spiritual and democratic religion of Russia, strengthened by union with the practical and organised religion of Rome' as a real possibility for overcoming the great schism between East and West, which would in turn allow the two provinces of the 'Ecclesia Anglicana' to take their 'proper place as two provinces of the Western Patriarchate'. He also saw the war as making it possible that the Holy Land and Constantinople would be recovered 'for Christian Sovereignty'.[29] That it was eventually a British army which marched into Jerusalem was a cause for jubilation and, for *The Messenger's* editor, of hope for the future.[30] Indeed, the war was itself a spur to the reunion of the Churches: 'Britain is no longer an island and never will be again. We have till the end of the war to teach our congregations and to prepare for reunion with European Catholics.'[31]

Despite the war, and despite the hostility of bishops, the ordinary life of the Catholic League carried on unabated. On 7 February 1914 a sodality for priests was inaugurated, under the patronage of the sixteenth-century saint Charles Borromeo, the Sodality of the Most Precious Blood. Over 30 priests joined immediately, undertaking to say each day the Roman Catholic version of the Divine Office (known as the Breviary), make an annual retreat and to remain celibate. Dues were collected, 'the annual shilling'. The Revd E. S. Maltby, who had taken over from Langford James as Superior General, retired from the office citing pressures of work, to be replaced by Fr W. J. Scott. A year later Fr Scott resigned, saying that his out-of-London commitments made it impossible to give enough time to the League. The decision was made not to appoint a new Superior General, but to have an 'anonymous' group leadership. This group included Fynes Clinton who, having changed dioceses, considered himself no longer bound by the requirement that he resign from the League and had rejoined. He eventually emerged as the sole 'Priest Director'.

---

29 Ibid., April/June 1916.

30 Ibid., January/March 1918. A 'crusade of prayer' had been launched 'for the restoration of the Holy Places to Christian Sovereignty'.

31 Ibid., April/June 1916.

The League was able to hold an annual 'Festa' as near as possible to the date of its foundation. These were gatherings which combined business with liturgy and always had a strong social and celebratory element. A much appreciated preacher on the first of these occasions was Ronald Arbuthnot Knox. He was a member though, he claimed in his early autobiography *A Spiritual Aeneid,* not a very active member: 'I have a horror of shilling subscriptions and weekly collects'. He had not, for example, attended the service at Corringham, 'a sort of devotional picnic ... with every circumstance of Mariolatry', but after the Bishop of St Albans banned Fynes Clinton and Langford James from officiating in his diocese, Knox wrote to him asking what his attitude was towards Knox himself who, as chaplain to Trinity College, Oxford, sometimes helped out at a mission in West Ham, then within the St Albans diocese. He was informed he would have to resign from the Catholic League or be banned: he refused to resign and found himself banned not only from the St Albans diocese but from that of Chelmsford as well – before 1914 part of St Albans. He also felt that, as a member of the League, he could not preach in Manchester while his father Edmund, a prominent Anglican Evangelical, was its bishop.[32] In 1917 Knox became a Roman Catholic – he was ordained an RC priest the following year.

The response of the General Secretary, Rivers Moore, to Knox's action illustrates the League's stance at that time towards Roman Catholicism:

The principle involved lies at the very foundation of the claim of the Church of England to be the Catholic Church of this country. 'Catholic' means 'universal' in the sense 'for all'. The Catholic Church must provide for the spiritual needs of every temperament and must be capable of developing every talent to the utmost. As surely as any local church says to a man 'I have no room for you. I cannot use your gifts', that

---

32 Ronald Knox, *A Spiritual Aeneid* (London: Burns and Oates, 1950), pp. 132–3: this is a second edition, the first being published in 1918 shortly after Knox had become a Roman Catholic. In his introduction to the new edition, 'After 33 Years', he indicates that little has changed in the text.

church is less than Catholic, is encouraging schism and is driving men to heresy. Further, this suggestion that English-men can be divided into two groups, one to be catered for by Canterbury and the other by Westminster, is a direct justi-fication of the presence of the Roman hierarchy and implies the acceptance of a permanent divided jurisdiction and con-flicting obedience. A logical extension of the principle would lead to a separate communion for every clique that chose to support a bishop.

The question that must be faced, and not only faced but answered quickly, is – How is the Church of England to become at once truly catholic and truly national? How can she retain, develop and use the special gifts of all her children, not merely the Celtic and Anglo-Saxon groups with which she has chiefly to deal on this island, but the thousand different mentalities and temperaments that might be united in her service throughout the British Empire? How is she to preserve untarnished the jewel of her national characteristics, which we are rightly told it is her part to contribute to the adornment of the heavenly Jerusalem, while avoiding every bar to reunion with other national Churches from which she was unwillingly separated?[33]

Rivers Moore, it seems from this passage, regarded the Roman Catholic Church in Britain – Westminster – as an interloper. Those with whom at this stage of its existence the Catholic League was seeking reunion, it would therefore appear, were not the Roman Catholics of Great Britain, but those on the Continent of Europe.[34]

---

33 *The Messenger*, October/December 1917.

34 Cf. Curtis, *Paul Couturier*, pp. 192–3: 'Moreover Anglican Papalism at its best has faced honestly and in a Christian way the relation of the Anglican Church to English Roman Catholics. It holds strongly that the Catholic Church in England bifurcated in the sixteenth century; that the true Church of England in our times is not merely the Church of England by law established, but is the Catholic Church in our land as a whole, albeit at present outwardly divided; that the Roman Church in England is not an intruded schismatic body, but the other section, so to speak, of the pre-Reformation English Church. This section inherits the view held by the great majority of the ecclesiastical lawyers who accepted the full claims of Papal

In the course of an exchange in the letter columns of the *Church Times* during July 1924, one correspondent signing him (or her) self simply an 'Inquirer' highlighted the anomaly of this position:

> The letters published in your recent issues from the Catholic League and Mr. C. G. Harrison bring into prominence a difficult question, on which many of us would like more information. It is common ground to both parties, and to Anglo-Catholics generally, that the Church of Rome is part of the true Church. Yet Mr. Harrison says that the Roman doctrine of the Pope is a 'blasphemous heresy.' But, as we have so often been told, this doctrine of the Pope is to the Roman Church a vital article of faith, which could no more be surrendered than the doctrine of the Incarnation or of the Trinity. Every member of the Roman Church is therefore committed to what, in Mr. Harrison's words, is a blasphemous heresy. Can such a body possibly be regarded as holding the 'one Faith'? I understand that on Anglo-Catholic principles it is the duty of a person born in a Roman Catholic country to submit to the Roman Church. But can it ever be the duty of anyone knowingly to adhere to a body which teaches a blasphemous heresy? Surely the Faith is not a matter of geography.[35]

---

authority. Anglican Catholics have their own antecedents in the upholders of the conciliar movement of the fifteenth century and those who inherited their doctrine. These believed in certain powers inherent in local churches which may have to be exercised. They held that the Papacy is of the bene *esse*, or rather in a sense of the *esse* of the Church, but is not essential to her very existence and may in case of necessity be disobeyed. As the great Gerson wrote, "The end of all laws not merely human but divine, is love which brings about unity. If therefore there be a case in which the observances of any law would dissolve unity and hinder the public safety, what sane man would say that it is desirable to observe it?" The claim, implied in all seriousness in some Anglican writing, and in common conversation flippantly by the harmful phrase "the Italian Mission", that Anglicans are the sole descendants of the pre-Reformation Church, is insupportable, if not ridiculous. The weakest point in much Catholic Anglicanism has been its failure to understand and to esteem English Roman Catholicism.'

35 *Church Times*, 25 July 1924.

2

Early Battles

In July 1918 the General Secretary decided it was appropriate to publish in *The Messenger* a description of the aims and purposes of the League. Its three objects were, he stated,

1 The promotion of fellowship among Catholics, and the Re-union of Christendom.
2 The Conversion of the world to the Catholic religion.
3 The Sanctification of our members.

In practice, however, much of its time, and space in its journal, were taken up with accounts of clergy, often members of the League, who were being deprived of their livings by their bishops, usually because of the introduction into their churches of the service of Benediction. Fr Reginald Wynter of St John's, Taunton, was mentioned in the 'General Secretary's Notes' for April/June 1920. When the Bishop of Bath and Wells had made a visitation to St John's a year earlier, Wynter and his church-wardens absented themselves – 'contumaciously' thought the bishop. He declared:

> I hereby forbid the Rev. Reginald Wynter, as vicar of this parish, to hold, or to allow to be held in this church, the service of Benediction, or any service or part of a service of the same nature. I further direct him to submit to me, for approval or otherwise, any service he desires to hold in this church other than services which are in the Book of Common Prayer, or those for which I or other lawful authority have given general permission to use in this diocese. I have to request the churchwardens, as my officers, to report to me if any such unauthorized services are held in this church. This

is my order and direction to the Rev. Reginald Wynter as vicar of this parish. I give this further order and direction to the churchwardens, and to each of them, and unless within six months from this date a confirmatory faculty shall have been obtained for the retention of the following articles, these articles be removed from the church, namely: The stoup, apparently for holy water, near the church door; the tabernacle on the principal holy table; the two additional holy tables; and the image of the Virgin Mary. As to other objects in this church which have been illegally introduced, I, for the moment, give no special directions. I also direct that no tabernacle or image nor other ornaments or decorations be in future placed in this church unless sanctioned by faculty. This is my further order and direction. It is my desire that these, my orders and directions, shall be strictly observed, and I earnestly impress upon all concerned the necessity for faithfully carrying them out.[1]

Wynter refused to mend his ways and, as the General Secretary remarked, was subsequently ejected from his living at about the same time as was his acquaintance, the somewhat eccentric Revd L. S. Wason, perpetual curate of Cury-with-Gunwalloe, by his diocesan, the Bishop of Truro.[2]

The Catholic League had perforce become something not listed among the General Secretary's description of its objects, a support group for clergy in trouble with their bishops. 'Our position as Catholics', Kenneth Ingram said in a lecture reported in *The Messenger* for July/September 1924, 'is essentially that of missionaries in a foreign land of prejudice and misunderstanding and ignorance'. Even the Priest Director – or especially the Priest Director – encountered the prejudice when, in 1921, Henry Fynes Clinton became rector of St Magnus the Martyr in Lower Thames Street, near London Bridge in the

---

1 *Church Times*, 11 July 1919.

2 See Roy Tricker, *Mr Wason ... I Think* (Leominster: Gracewing, 1994). One of the photographs in this book shows Wason apparently playing tennis is his biretta. Fr Peter Blagdon-Gamlen preached a sermon on Sandys Wason at Gunwalloe in 1992 which gave a brief account of his life and quoted some of his poetry. It appeared in *The Messenger* for October 1992.

City of London, together with the two other parishes linked to this living: St Michael, Crooked Lane, and St Margaret, New Fish Street. He found St Magnus the Martyr a rather bleak building, decorated with no Christian symbols: it resembled, he said, a synagogue,[3] and immediately embarked embellishments. To the standard, and sparsely attended, Church of England services he added Roman-style ones. Congregations increased, but so did complaints. Some churchwardens at the church, 'of the Kensit faction' opined *The Messenger*, were trying to get the tabernacle removed so Fynes launched the 'St Magnus Guard of Honour'. They were to 'defend by all right means' the tabernacle, and 'to manifest publicly and increase' devotion to the Sacrament therein.

The Bishop of London was in a quandary. Clearly Fynes was making a success of the church, not least by holding well-attended lunch-time services, at the time very much a rarity, but in the Diocesan Chancellor's view some of the changes Fynes had introduced smacked of Romanism. He ordered the removal of various items including a crucifix and a holy water stoup. 'A defence fund will probably have to be raised', said *The Messenger*, meanwhile Fynes 'in reparation' invented yet another guild, the Confraternity 'de Salve Regina' (the English prayer/hymn 'Hail, Holy Queen'), with a committee very grandly entitled the Grand Court of the Fraternity, to pray regularly in front of the Lady statue.[4] The next issue of *The Messenger* reported on 'The Spoliation of St Magnus'. The case against the Chancellor had been taken to the King's Bench and had been lost, with costs awarded against the League. Subsequently, on the instruction of the bishop, the tabernacle was removed, as was the sanctuary lamp, 'dragged down by a churchwarden'.

It is difficult to avoid the impression that Fynes, backed by the Catholic League, was enjoying the battle. On Christmas

---

3 Salter, *The Anglican Papalist*, p. 89. The details of the subsequent controversy, only summarized here, are to be found in *The Anglican Papalist*, pp. 89–108.

4 *The Messenger*, April/June 1922. Strictly speaking it was a reinvention, since the Confraternity had originally been founded in the fourteenth century, only the second of such guilds to be established in the city of London. It is still active.

Eve 1923 he appealed to the Chancellor's Court for the embellishments by Martin Travers mentioned in the opening paragraph of this book. Not all those requested were approved, but most were despite the continued complaints of one of his churchwardens. Almost exactly a year later, on 15 December 1924, the Bishop of London, Arthur Winnington-Ingram, performed an opening ceremony for the refurbished St Magnus. Yet less than a week after that Fynes was in trouble again. Someone had sent to the bishop a prayer card which had been left before a statue of the Virgin. The prayer was innocuous enough, but in the small print at the bottom were the words '300 days indulgence, plenary once a month'. The bishop must surely have been heartily tired of the affairs of St Magnus. He wrote to Fynes saying that no prayer should be used that had not first received his approval, and as for indulgences, 'we do not talk about "indulgences" in the Church of England'. Fynes excused himself saying that the prayer card had been bought in a Roman Catholic bookshop.[5]

Fynes remained as rector of St Magnus until his death in December 1959, but other members of the Catholic League were far less lucky, and were deprived of their living, sometimes for the style of their services, but also simply for having a tabernacle, as in the story above of Reginald Wynter. There was a particular hostility on the part of the bishops of the day to the service of Benediction, and *The Messenger* came to its defence in an article which was based on the Church of England's own canon law. It declared that any procedure against a priest held under the 1840 Clergy Discipline Act could not be recognized because any court established for the purpose drew its authority from an act of Parliament and was therefore not a spiritual court. The article went on to argue that opposition to the act of adoration involved in the service of Benediction was tantamount to denying the presence of Christ in the Eucharist. But it also pointed out that the Church's own canons permitted Benediction, at the very least on particular occasions. There was, however, in June 1924, a much more fundamental attack

---

5 Salter, *The Anglican Papalist*, pp. 107–08.

on the theological position of the Catholic League, and from a source which the League might otherwise have considered to be friendly.

The problem arose because of the League's decision as to what would constitute its profession of faith. Clearly it was necessary for the organization to have some statement of its basic convictions and of its main purposes. The purposes it defined as '(1) to restore to England that part of her heritage which she lost through the reformation; (2) to form a nucleus of faithful Catholics to withstand the heresies of the day, and (3) to be ready for united action in any great emergencies'. It was necessary, therefore, that the League's members should all have a 'working knowledge' of the Catholic faith such 'as a child brought up in a Catholic school would possess, and this without any reservation'. The committee decided in 1920 that this should be the creed of the Council of Trent, which, it was claimed, 'aptly summarises the Faith of the Pre-Reformation Church of England'. The problem, of course, was that the Tridentine creed was very much a post-Reformation credo, so the committee explained that the Church, though in origin divine, was constituted by members who were human, and by the sixteenth century there was a real need of reformation, which was 'accomplished by the Church herself in the Council of Trent, and also by a party of irresponsible Germans such as Luther and his associates'. Postulants were to be asked to sign this declaration of faith before being admitted to full membership.[6]

It was evident to all that this sixteenth-century reforming Council was unquestionably Roman Catholic, as therefore was its creed: 'There are still many people calling themselves Catholics to whom the word "Rome" inspires terror and dislike – is it possible there are some in the Catholic League? It is not a spirit to be proud of.'[7] This obvious fact, that the League had embraced a Roman Catholic credo, had been seized upon by the League's critics – in, for example, the clash between Fynes Clinton (who, as if to prove his credentials as a true

6 *The Messenger*, April/June 1920.
7 Ibid., January/March 1921.

Catholic, had on 23 October 1920 at Holy Trinity, Hoxton, inaugurated the Rosary Confraternity of the Sacred Hearts of Jesus and Mary) and the Bishop of London. The League's committee was not deterred, and a section-by-section explanation of the Tridentine creed was published in successive issues of *The Messenger*.

It came under attack when, in June 1924, the English Church Union[8] held its annual meeting at Church House, Westminster. The distinguished theologian Canon William Sparrow Simpson proposed the motion:

The Union, celebrating, its sixty-fifth anniversary, ninety-one years since the beginning, of the Oxford Movement, fifty years after the passing of the Public Worship Regulation Act, records its devout thankfulness to the Great Head of the Church, for the blessing which has rested on its work, despite penal laws, persecution and imprisonments. The Union further expresses its profound sense of the momentous nature of the task to which it is dedicated – namely, that of maintaining the position of the Church of England as an integral part of the whole Catholic Church of Christ, and its consequent: determination to spare no efforts in the cause of Catholic Truth.

He then went on, in a speech reported, apparently more or less verbatim, in the *Church Times* for 27 June, to explain at length the second part of his motion.

In the course of his address, Canon Simpson took the Anglo-Catholic movement to task because, he said,

Attention was being concentrated on psychological facts, the character of the music, dignity and impressiveness; every detail of the ceremonial was carefully thought out. Every detail of the sermon was not. The appeal was aesthetic rather than intellectual, devotional rather than dogmatic.

---

8 Whenever the League had challenged the authority of civil courts to determine matters the League regarded as spiritual, it was relying on the advice, and the arguments, of the English Church Union.

The intention was to create an atmosphere, to cultivate reverence, to develop the devotional capacity and by those means to mature the soul. That method was being rewarded with remarkable success, but regarded from the intellectual side there were grounds for uneasiness. There were Catholics whose knowledge of doctrine was small; they seemed ruled by devotional or ceremonial interest, and at times there was a startling disregard of profound dogmatic differences. Dogmas appeared to be ignored, or, if recognized, swallowed rather than understood. There was a large amount of unintelligent religion, and that occurred not only in the case of illiterate people but in persons whose education qualified them to make more use of their reason.[9]

While these strictures might be widely applied, he went on to criticize Anglican Papalists, almost, but not quite, mentioning in the process the Catholic League itself:

The resolution maintained the position of the Church of England as an integral part of the whole Catholic Church of Christ, and that was an important proposition. For the sake of everyone concerned it was well to explain what that meant, because there were many who did not understand what the Church of England represented. The resolution went on to speak of the determination to spare no efforts in the cause of Catholic truth. They must explain what they meant by Catholic truth, especially as there was a society which adopted the name which would certainly not agree with that resolution. By Catholic truth the resolution must mean the doctrine which was accepted by the entire Catholic Church, by the East as well as by the West, and not that doctrine which was accepted by one portion and rejected by another. And to affirm that the Church of England was an integral part of the whole Catholic Church was to affirm

---

9 *Church Times*, 27 June 1924. The whole text is in reported speech, which makes it slightly more difficult to grasp than it probably was at the time.

that the Catholic Faith, sacraments and ministry, existed in a communion in which the Papal authority had no place.[10]

While, as remarked above, Sparrow Simpson did not name the Catholic League, there could have been little doubt that he was referring to it. In a leader in the same issue, however, the *Church Times* had no such inhibitions:

The Anglo-Catholic, therefore, who, generally under the cloak of anonymity, seeks to identify the movement with everything that is Roman, including the full Papal claims, is far worse than an eccentric. He is an enemy to the cause that he seeks to serve. A correspondent draws attention this week to a pamphlet issued by a body calling itself the Catholic League, in which it is explained that members of the League must subscribe to the Creed of the Council of Trent, acknowledging the Pope as 'Successor of St. Peter, Prince of the Apostles, and Vicar of Jesus Christ.' We say, without hesitation, that no loyal English Churchman can subscribe to this declaration of faith. We do not overestimate the importance of the Catholic League, but Fr. Cornibeer[11] warned the E.C.U. that in the provinces the Catholic movement is hampered and checked by the irresponsible 'spike,' and we constantly hear the same complaint from our correspondents. The Catholic laity is English. It respects order and authority. It resents freakish religion.

Anglican Papalism of the Catholic League variety, it would seem, represented for the *Church Times* a 'freakish religion'.

Yet otherwise the weekly appeared not unsympathetic to the League, and on another page printed an appeal by the rector, Henry Fynes Clinton, and the churchwardens of St Magnus the Martyr for money to pay for the defence of the church in

---

10 Ibid.

11 A. E. Cornibeer was vicar of St Mathew's, Westminster, an Anglo-Catholic parish where Frank Weston, the Bishop of Zanzibar mentioned earlier, had once been a curate and where Spencer Jones had delivered his lecture on 'England and the Holy See' (see above, p. 4).

the controversy recounted above.[12] The paper had, after all, been founded in 1863 'to promote the interests of the Catholic revival within the Church of England', as one of its more recent editors pointed out.[13] It was not surprising, then, that it gave space to the League's Secretary, Mr L. G. Fisher, to answer the League's critics.

Canon Sparrow Simpson's most serious criticism was implied in the sentence, 'By Catholic truth the resolution must mean the doctrine which was accepted by the entire Catholic Church, by the East as well as by the West, and not that doctrine which was accepted by one portion and rejected by another.' The *Church Times* leader made the same argument. But, went on Canon Simpson, the status of the papacy was accepted by only one part of the Catholic Church, therefore it could not be part of Catholic truth. Fisher's response was to claim that it would be in practice quite impossible to base one's convictions on whatever doctrines the Eastern and Western Churches held in common. 'This is indefinite and unworkable', Fisher asserted, 'because it necessitates examination of vast literature, for which few are competent, and those that are have no authority to impose their conclusions even if they agree.' He defended the use of the Tridentine creed on the grounds that, as an entirely voluntary organization, the League could choose what rules were to be observed, that there was a need for a clear statement of belief, the lack of which he asserted 'was the chief weakness of the English Church', and that the 'Creed has been adopted as the best Expression of what was the pre-Reformation Faith of the Church of England, i.e., of the only times when she possessed one mind in faith'.[14] That the creed was self-evidently a post-Reformation document he clearly thought to be of no consequence.

These controversies absorbed the energy and the finances of the Catholic League and, of the latter, the League had little

---

12 Cf. p. 22f.

13 Bernard Palmer, *Gadfly for God: A History of the Church Times* (London: Hodder and Stoughton, 1991), p. 2.

14 *Church Times*, 11 July 1924, under the curious heading 'Henry VI or Henry VIII?'

enough and was constantly appealing for money. Membership cost only a shilling a year (badge six pence extra). Apart from printing and dispatching *The Messenger*, expenses were few, though from 1923 onwards there was also an office to pay for, originally at 32 Finsbury Square and from 1927 until the outbreak of the Second World War, when it was given up, at 11 City Road.[15] There was a multiplicity of different funds, including 'The Tabernacle Treasury' for 'donations to maintain the dignity and the cult of the Blessed Sacrament' and a Chantry Fund to support requiem Masses for deceased members. Each of the various associated bodies such as the Apostleship of Prayer had their membership fee, albeit modest, and usually a badge. Badges were to be worn at least in processions, but members of the Rosary Confraternity of the Sacred Hearts of Jesus and Mary were expected to wear a mantle coloured white in honour of Our Lady, with a red collar, red in honour of the Sacred Heart. It cost 30 shillings, but purchasers were assured it was made of 'durable material that can be cleansed'.[16]

These accoutrements, together with a Catholic League veil for women members, were on show at the annual Festa. At first the Festa was held at different locations, but in 1920 *The Messenger* announced that through the kindness of Fr Tooth the celebrations would be held in the convent grounds at Woodside, near Croydon – a timetable of trains and buses was appended. Arthur Tooth, a member of the Society of the Holy Cross, became a hero among Anglo-Catholics for having been briefly imprisoned in January 1877, basically for contempt of court, after repeatedly refusing to recognize the authority of the Court of Arches where he had been prosecuted for the use of incense and the wearing of vestments. On his release, he returned briefly to St James', Hatcham, in the south-east of London, in which parish he had ministered with great success since 1868, but had resigned his living in 1878 and never held another post with direct cure of souls. In that same year, 1878, he purchased the property at Woodside on which he started a boys' school, an orphanage and a convent. In 1927, he moved

---

15 Doolan, *The First Fifty Years*, p. 17.
16 *The Messenger*, April/June 1920.

the convent and school to Otford in Kent where the school – St Michael's – still survives. Woodside, then Otford Court, became the regular venues for the annual celebrations.[17]

Another annual event was the pilgrimage to Walsingham, made for the first time by a group of priests in 1926. The shrine of Our Lady in this small Norfolk town claims to date from 1061, when the Lady of the Manor said she had seen a vision of the house in Palestine where the Annunciation occurred: she had a wooden replica built, which became a major centre of pilgrimage not just in England but from the Continent as well. It was destroyed during the Reformation (despite the fact that Henry VIII himself had come on pilgrimage), but with the blessing of Pope Leo XIII devotion to the shrine was restored by Roman Catholics in 1897, not in Walsingham itself but in the RC church in nearby Kings Lynn: the statue, carved in Oberammergau, was based on a picture in the Roman church of Santa Maria in Cosmedin.[18] A year earlier Charlotte Pearson Boyd,[19] who had been received in the Roman Catholic Church in 1894, bought what is now known as the Slipper Chapel,[20] had it restored, then gave it, with an endowment, to the Benedictine community at Downside Abbey. Or tried to do so. Walsingham lay in the RC diocese of Northampton, and its bishop at the time was opposed to the Benedictines running a shrine or to allowing Mass to be celebrated there. Instead, in August 1897 there was a pilgrimage to Walsingham starting

---

17 In the October/December 1953 issue of *The Messenger*, Fynes Clinton wrote of Arthur Tooth that he was 'the last surviving victim. He appeared on the platform of the first Anglo-Catholic Congress [in 1920] and received a great ovation. What they went through saving for us what is now taken for granted, is now largely forgotten, and the principles fought for abandoned by modern ritualists who are content to enjoy the results.'

18 It had been the titular church of Cardinal Reginald Pole, the last Roman Catholic Archbishop of Canterbury. See Charles Smith, *A Pocket Guide to Walsingham* (London: Mowbray, 1988), p. 11.

19 See the pamphlet by Ethel M. Hostler, *Charlotte Boyd: Some Notes on Her Life*, published as a supplement to the February/March issue of *The Messenger*, 1996.

20 The origin of the name is uncertain. It may come from 'slype', meaning a way through, or it may indicate that it was at this point medieval pilgrims removed their shoes to walk the last mile in bare feet.

out from the RC shrine in Kings Lynn. Mass was not cele-brated in the Slipper Chapel until 1934.[21]

In the meantime, Alfred Hope Patten had come to Walsing-ham as vicar of the Church of England parish. He arrived in 1921 and immediately set about reviving devotion to Our Lady of Walsingham in his church. He installed a shrine, with a statue based on a seal in the British Museum. This did not please the lords of the manor of Walsingham, and in particular it did not please the Bishop of Norwich in whose (C of E) diocese Hope Patten's church lay. Bishop Bertram Pollock does not receive particularly favourable treatment in accounts of the re-estab-lishment of the cult of Our Lady of Walsingham, yet before becoming a bishop he had been headmaster of Wellington Col-lege, and the author, diplomat and politician Harold Nicolson, who had been a student at the school during Pollock's period of office, wrote very highly of him. 'Opposition to the honour given to Our Lady at Walsingham', noted *The Messenger* for April/June 1931, 'long expected by those who know the way of the enemy has been stirred up and the Bishop has felt it incumbent on him to demand the removal of the shrine from the church.' The shrine was indeed eventually moved out of the church and re-erected at the other end of the village in a newly built chapel with 15 altars, one for each of the 'mysteries' of the rosary. The new church, with the Holy House beside it, was not located on ecclesiastical property, so Hope Patten and Fynes Clinton had a free hand. Fynes took particular charge of the altar dedicated to the 'mystery' The Death on the Cross and placed it under the patronage of the Catholic League: he installed a statue of Our Lady of Victories, the League's patron. For the formal opening of the shrine on 15 October 1931, a special train was hired to carry pilgrims from London to Walsingham.

Fynes was closely allied with Hope Patten, and his influence is particularly to be seen in the Latin inscription on the founda-tion stone of the new shrine, which reads in part that it was laid

---

21 Hostler, *Charlotte Boyd*, pp. 10–11. The first permanent RC priest to be appointed was Bruno Scott James. It was not a very diplomatic choice as he had been for several years a monk of Nashdom and there was for some time tension between the two shrines.

in 1931, 'the ninth year of the Pontificate of our most holy Lord Pius XI ... Bertram being Bishop of the Church of Norwich and Hope Patten the Parish Priest of Walsingham'. Hope Patten was not a learned man, so the wording was undoubtedly that of Fynes Clinton. Bishop Pollock was outraged at being subordinated to the Pope and demanded that his name be erased. It was therefore cemented over, but after his death in 1943 the cement was removed, leaving his name, untouched for well over a decade by wind or rain, rather more visible than that of Pius XI or Hope Patten. Because the shrine was no longer on Church of England property, a board of trustees had to be created to take charge of it. The trustees were, and are, called the College of Guardians, and number 20 in all, including both priests and laity, though the Master of the College has to be a priest. In 1933, Fynes Clinton presented the Master with a silver-gilt chain of office; from 1938, when attending the shrine all Guardians wore a blue velvet mantle and, from 1947, a star on a ribbon around their necks.[22]

Fynes, who was, inevitably, one of the Guardians, was a keen promoter of pilgrimage to Walsingham. He led a small pilgrimage there in 1922, not as a member of the Catholic League but as chaplain to the League of Our Lady. Very few people joined in, but in Walsingham itself the villagers made up the numbers and proved themselves for the most part enthusiastic supporters of Hope Patten's restored shrine, in subsequent years providing free accommodation to pilgrims. The first strictly Catholic League pilgrimage took place in 1927, numbering some 30 people, priests and laity – there had been one the year before of priests alone, from the League and from the Sodality of the Precious Blood. From then on, they became annual events. The July/September 1928 issue of *The Messenger* contained an account of that year's pilgrimage, which took place on 19–21 June; to explain the decline in numbers attending, the editor noted that the dates were not as convenient as the previous year's pilgrimage, which had taken place during Whit Week:

---

22 For this section on Walsingham, see Salter, *The Anglican Papalist*, pp. 112–17; Yelton, *Anglican Papalism*, pp. 130–41.

Our Pilgrimage started with Mass and the Blessing of Pilgrims at St Magnus' by London Bridge, and those who came from London caught the 3 o'clock from King's Cross and on arrival at Fakenham cars were waiting to take us the five miles to Walsingham Church, where we met other pilgrims from all parts. Met by the rector at the doors, we immediately paid a first visit to the shrine which is in the chapel of the Church where the Blessed Sacrament is reserved. One of the great lessons brought before us is the close union of devotion to Our Lady with the Blessed Sacrament, and throughout the pilgrimage this thought is much brought to the front.

After this supper is served at the Hospice of Our Lady Star of the Sea, kept by the Sisters of St Peter's, Horbury, and everything is exceedingly well arranged.

The Pilgrimage was under the direction of Fr Fynes Clinton, who based his addresses on the first Pilgrimage to our Lady: that of the Shepherds at Bethlehem.

Going on pilgrimage was regarded as a very 'Catholic' thing to do, and was presented as such, but it appeared to have raised few hackles. The *Church Times* carried several accounts of such visits to shrines, and especially to Walsingham, most of these narratives somewhat longer than that in *The Messenger*, and more vivid. These accounts, however, were all associated with the League of Our Lady rather than with the Catholic League.

There were, naturally, pilgrimages of members of the Catholic League to other centres of Catholic devotion, not least to Rome itself: Fynes Clinton led one which set out from Magnus the Martyr on 30 August 1926 and travelled to Rome by way of Paris and the church there of Our Lady of Victories. The objects of the group were, according to *The Messenger*, '(a) The worship of God in the honouring of the Shrines of His Saints and the seat of His Prince Apostle; (b) Intercession for Reunion of England with the Holy See; (c) Reparation for the schism of the XVI century; (d) lastly, each has his own private intentions and those committed to him by others for prayer'.[23]

---

23 *The Messenger*, October/December 1926.

3

How to be Catholic

The pilgrimage to Rome came in the hiatus in the Malines Conversations which followed the death in January 1926 of Cardinal Désiré-Félicien-François-Joseph Mercier, the Archbishop of Malines and an early enthusiast for the union of the Churches, and the appointment of his somewhat less ecumenically minded successor Archbishop (not yet Cardinal) Jozef-Ernest van Roey.[1] In England Cardinal Bourne, the Archbishop of Westminster, had unexpectedly shown himself sympathetic to the series of meetings at Malines (Mechelen), but any hopes of a breakthrough were undermined by the Rome-based English Benedictine Cardinal Gasquet, a clutch of English Jesuits and the editor of the Catholic weekly, *The Tablet*, Ernest Oldmeadow.[2] The Catholic League appeared to show little interest in these meetings – at least, none that is recorded apart from calling for prayers in the October/December 1926 issue of *The Messenger* for the renewal of the conversations in 1927, which proved to be the last in the series. Alongside this it published a letter dated October 1925 from Mercier to Randall Davidson, the Archbishop of Canterbury: 'not only have our meetings brought hearts together', wrote the cardinal, 'which is already an appreciated result, but that they

---

1 For an account, see John A. Dick, *The Malines Conversations Revisited* (Leuven: Leuven University Press, 1989). Van Roey did, however, continue the conversations for one more session, and had earlier presented a paper entitled 'The Episcopate and the Papacy from the Theological Point of View' (Dick, *The Malines Conversations Revisited*, p. 139).

2 It was Oldmeadow's two-volume biography of Bourne (*Francis Cardinal Bourne*, London: Burns, Oates and Washbourne, 1940) that gave the erroneous impression the English cardinal had opposed the conversations.

have also on important points harmonized our thoughts and achieved progress in agreement'.

The relative silence of the League is all the more surprising because Dom Lambert Beauduin, who at the time was lecturing on ecclesiology at Sant'Anselmo, the Benedictine College in Rome, had at the request of Mercier submitted a paper to the participants in the conversations, which was to form the basis of his later book *L'Eglise Anglicane unie non absorbée*.[3] He was proposing that the Archbishopric of Canterbury should be considered a patriarchate along the lines of the Uniate Churches of the East – he had a particular interest in Eastern Christianity – which would allow the Church of England to maintain its own liturgy and canon law. As it was contrary to canon law that there should be two competing Catholic hierarchies in England, argued Beauduin, the Roman Catholic hierarchy would have to be suppressed – not surprisingly something which, when they came to hear of it, the English RC bishops scarcely viewed with equanimity.[4] Many members of the Catholic League, on the other hand, saw the 'Uniate' status of Canterbury as a very viable way forward in their commitment to corporate reunion of the two Churches.

In the April 1971 issue of *The Messenger*, there was a curious coda to this story provided by E. J. Pizey who described himself

---

3 Published at Malines, 1977. The paper was read out at Malines by Mercier, without revealing the author: Van Roey identified him in 1930. Beauduin (1873–1960) had been a monk at the monastery of Mont César, Louvain, where he had come under the influence of the Irish-born prior, Dom (now Blessed) Columba Marmion. He later founded a monastery at Amay-sur-Meuse, near Liège, dedicated to ecumenical relations between Western and Eastern Christianity, but his radical views on ecumenism, coloured perhaps by his stay in England as an army chaplain during the First World War, brought about first his exile (1928) and then his condemnation by Rome (1931). From then on, he turned his attention to the liturgy rather than ecumenism. In 1945, the condemnation was removed thanks to the intervention of his friend Angelo Roncalli, the future Pope John XXIII, and he was able to return to his monastery, located since 1939 at Chevetogne, south-east of Brussels. See Dick, *The Malines Conversations Revisited*, p. 234.

4 Though there is a suggestion that Bourne at least was willing to consider it, cf. Dick, *The Malines Conversations Revisited*, p. 137.

in the course of his short contribution as 'probably the League's oldest life member' and a dedicated ecumenist 'among Catholics all around the world (as my passport shows)'. He claimed that the Roman Catholic author Robert Sencourt[5] had, through the good offices of Lord Halifax, been appointed a private emissary from Pope Pius XI to the priests of the Catholic League. The chief obstacle to unity with the Church of England was, according to this version of events, the Holy Office,[6] which had 'closed down the Malines Conversations against His Holiness's wishes'. What Pius XI wanted, Pizey laid out:

That the Church of England be a Corporate body in union with His Holiness directly, on the following basic principles:
(i) Service in the Vernacular on the basis of the (1662) Book of Common Prayer
(ii) Communion in both kinds
(iii) Married clergy to be accepted
(iv) Varied standards of ceremonial ranging from Lights and Coloured Stoles, without vestments to the full standard of the Ornaments Rubric
(v) Re-ordination not necessary. Orders can be regularized or confirmed.

Sencourt was, according to Pizey, surprised that the Catholic League knew nothing of this because the Pope had written to the Archbishop of Canterbury with these proposals. Pizey believed that they were not taken further because 'As the B.C.P. was in disfavour at St Magnus the Martyr, it was coldly received, and no reply was sent to His Holiness.'

The whole story is highly suspect. It is impossible to believe that the imperious Pope Pius would allow himself to be overruled by the Holy Office, that he would sweep aside Leo XIII's ruling on Anglican orders in *Apostolicae Curae*, that he would

---

5 Sencourt wrote a number of books on literary figures (he was a friend of T. S. Eliot) and on Spain, though he is best remembered, if remembered at all, by Roman Catholics as the author of *The Genius of the Vatican* (London: Jonathan Cape, 1935).

6 Formerly the Roman Inquisition, now the Congregation for the Doctrine of the Faith.

show no concern about the attitude of the English RC hierarchy or that one man, Henry Fynes Clinton, could single-handedly abort a papal initiative. Sencourt had a reputation as something of a fantasist, but Pizey clearly believed him, and the proposals he ascribed to Pius XI in the main reflected the vision of the Catholic League at the time. As Fynes often asserted, *'Our Schism from Rome was Corporate: the remedy must be Corporate.* Individual secession serves but to postpone reunion and leaves the problem where it was before.' The 'predisposing causes' of Henry VIII's break with Rome, he argued in *Centenary Tractate Number Eight – What Are We To Say?* 'were the corruption of Hildebrand's great ideal, of usurpation of secular power, of avarice and political intrigue'. He went on

> [Corporate reunion] need not mean the loss of all just Autonomy and her [the Church of England's] own Canon Law; perhaps there could be a jurisdiction for Canterbury analogous to that of the Eastern Patriarchates and on the other hand a partial decentralization of detailed administration from Rome, a desire for which is not unknown among loyal Roman Catholics. It is reasonable to believe that the re-conversion of England could best be effected by an English rite which could well be conceded.
>
> But it does mean the rectifying of the dislocation in the Apostolic College of the Catholic Episcopate.[7]

The last sentence is not a little opaque and is not explained in what follows in Fynes's text. The most obvious meaning, however, is that in the author's view the RC hierarchy in England would have to disappear to make way for the Uniate Patriarchate of Canterbury, a highly unrealistic expectation even if widely held. In 1935, when the canonizations of Thomas More and John Fisher coincided with the appointment of the

---

7 *The Messenger*, September 1983. The quotations from the *Centenary Tractate* occur in an article by Brooke Lunn, 'Father Fynes Clinton and Corporate Reunion'. The 'Centenary' was that of the sermon on 'National Apostasy' delivered by John Keble in July 1833, the event which is commonly taken to signal the start of the Oxford, or Tractarian, Movement.

remarkable Arthur Hinsley as successor to Cardinal Bourne as Archbishop of Westminster, an article in *The Messenger* entitled 'Our Other Half' set out to attenuate these views. The author suggested that the position of the 'sub-Tractarians', as he called them, could be turned against the Church of England: if one believed that the Church of Rome had intruded a hierarchy into a territory that was canonically that of the C of E, what of the C of E intruding its hierarchy into territory which was that of the Roman Catholics – he cited Western Canada, Australia and parts of Africa.[8] If the sub-Tractarian position was to be accepted, the article went on, then Roman Catholics in England were schismatics.

The solution, the author believed, was to look at what each Church had retained, and what each had lost. The Roman Catholic Church had kept its links to the Holy See and the rest of the Western Church; it had kept the ancient doctrines; it also had, with some small changes, kept the rites of the pre-Reformation Church. What it had lost was canonical continuity, and it was that which the Church of England had retained: 'And while we cling to our heritage of canonical continuity which they have lost, let us acknowledge that spiritual continuity which they share with us instead of holding them to be schismatics and calling them "the Italian Mission", as some do, a title which after all is equally applicable to ourselves.' Yet despite this argument, prejudices ran deep. As late as June 2006, *The Messenger* carried an article headed 'So where do we go from here? A personal view' by the Revd Canon F. E. Pickard in which he described the Roman Catholic Church as 'largely a Chaplaincy for the Émigré, and is unwilling/unable to minister to the unchurched English'.

The Malines conversations had a direct impact on another issue which preoccupied the Catholic League in its first two decades: the revision of the Prayer Book.[9] In a sense, the debate

---

8 Ancient canon law permitted only one hierarchy in a specific territory.

9 The account which follows is heavily dependent on John Maiden, *National Religion and the Prayer Book Controversy, 1927–1928* (Woodbridge: Boydell & Brewer, 2009). Maiden's narrative makes only a single passing reference to the Catholic League, which does not merit a mention in

should have passed the League's members, or many of them, by because they used either the Latin Roman missal or an English translation of it. But there were problems in the margins. Under the Public Worship Regulation Act of 1874 clergy could be prosecuted and ultimately imprisoned for ritualistic practices redolent of Catholicism. In the end, only five were ever sent to gaol, including Arthur Tooth who has been mentioned above,[10] but it was not repealed until 1965. It was, however, ineffective after the 1906 four-volume report of the Royal Commission on Ecclesiastical Discipline. The Royal Commission declared that the 1662 Prayer Book was too prescriptive and that changes should be made. They came slowly. In 1912 reservation of the Sacrament was permitted, though only for immediate use and for communion for the sick. This permission did not, however, envisage continuous reservation in a tabernacle, or services of adoration of the reserved Sacrament: as has been seen,[11] the service of Benediction of the Blessed Sacrament was a frequent cause of conflict between some bishops and their more Catholic-minded clergy.

The bishops of the Church of England were concerned to introduce a measure which would to some extent mollify such priests and thereby bring about a degree of discipline in liturgical practice. A meeting of the League on 1 July 1916 reported:

A discussion took place concerning the recent proposals made to adopt the Mass of the First Prayer Book [that of 1549, which was judged to be more 'Catholic'], or where that could not be done, the rearrangement of the prayers in the Prayer Book service to be more in accord with the ancient order. The priests present were unanimous that although from the purely liturgical point of view the 'Edward VI Mass' was no doubt much superior to that of the Prayer Book, yet the attempt to reintroduce a service which is wholly obsolete and never had any real authority either canonical or

---

the index. He remarks that the 'Anglo Papalists' were the least influential of the various groups opposing the revision (see p. 51).

10 P. 29.

11 Above, pp. 22.

of usage, would only bring in another division in practice among Catholics.[12]

The Great War had modified many people's views on rituals, and especially on prayers for the dead which were officially approved in 1919, and this changing liturgical climate encouraged the bishops to press ahead with a revision of the Prayer Book. They produced a revised version in 1923, but this pleased no one except themselves, and the various factions published their own proposals. The Catholic League felt itself under attack, chiefly on the grounds of reservation and Benediction. A parish in Fulham had its funds withdrawn by the bishop because of Benediction and could no longer support its curates. *The Messenger* published an appeal on the parish's behalf despite, as it was careful to point out, the unhealthy state of the League's own finances.[13]

As a long (for *The Messenger*) article in the January/March 1927 issue of the League's publication remarked, there was a strange belief that the revision would be welcomed by Catholics as it was based on the 1549 Prayer Book, which was more 'Catholic' than the 1552 or 1662 versions. This aroused the ire of the evangelicals who saw the revision in the light of the recently concluded Malines conversations and believed that the Church of England was being drawn Rome-ward and that the battle for the Reformation had once again to be joined.[14] It was 'the first step in the rapid subjugation of England to the power of Rome', declared the *English Churchman* on 20 January 1927. In an article in the same journal on 27 October, John Kensit warned, 'At the Reformation it was decided that any self-respecting nation could only have one head, that was supreme in all affairs within the realm, whether civil or ecclesiastical. And we turned out the Pope because he was a nuisance to the country. There is a danger of that position being reversed.'[15]

---

12 *The Messenger*, July/September 1916.
13 Ibid., July/September 1924.
14 Maiden, *National Religion*, p. 65.
15 Quoted, Maiden, *National Religion*, pp. 98 and 99.

It was the evangelicals' position, therefore, at least as enunciated by Kensit though there were other voices in a similar vein,[16] that in the revision the national identity was at stake and that sovereignty over the Church lay with Parliament. Such a view was obviously anathema to the League. Its members held firmly that the bishops of the Church of England, because state-appointed, had no authority to interfere with the Church's liturgy. 'It should be made clear that no [prayer] book is tolerable that imposes a new Canon for the Mass put together as the result of party compromise and lobbying, like a Railway Bill in parliament.'[17] Minor 'points to be watched' were

(a) The legalising of the use of surplice only in celebrating the Eucharist. This is to flout Catholic custom and emphasise our distinction from the rest of the Church.
(b) The inclusion in the Calendar of the names of persons never canonised, such as Cranmer and other protestants.
(c) The prohibition of devotions to the Blessed Sacrament reserved and the ordering of Reservation in two kinds, contrary to Catholic practice.[18]

One significant proposal for the 1927 revision, not mentioned in the Catholic League's protests, was the placing of the epiclesis, the prayer calling down the Holy Spirit on the bread and wine to be consecrated, after the words of institution, which undermined the conviction that it was the words of Christ at

---

16 Such as Bishop E. A. Knox, by this time (1926) retired from the see of Manchester: 'I am not going to apologise for saying that a national submission to the Church of Rome would be the losing of the nation's soul.' Quoted Maiden, *National Religion*, p. 75

17 *The Messenger*, January/March 1927.

18 Ibid. Cf. also Doolan, *The First Fifty Years*, p. 19. Rather oddly, in 1944 *The Messenger* expressed satisfaction that the bishops 'where they tolerate at all the Reservation of the Sanctissimum, to enforce the use of Aumbries in place of tabernacles or the Hanging Pyx, satisfaction so far as they are one with the medieval Popes! For the use of the Aumbry for this purpose was attempted by the Popes against the resistance of the English hierarchy and priests who persisted in using the hanging Pyx.' In fact, the use of the Aumbry had been mandated by the bishops in the rules for reservation both in the 1927 and the 1928 versions.

the Last Supper, repeated at the altar by the priest, that during Mass effected the consecration of the elements.[19]

When the bill came before Parliament in 1927 it was rejected in the House of Commons by 240 votes to 207. The bishops revised it slightly and presented it again in 1928. As the *Church Times* editorialized, 'At the eleventh hour there have been introduced into the rubrics new restrictions ... We are clear that the majority of Catholics will agree that the restrictions are intolerable. They evince a deplorable desire to placate Protestant prejudice and to retain the State connexion almost at any price. They weaken the authority of the Bishops. They make obedience difficult and loyalty necessarily qualified.'[20] For once the Catholic League and the *Church Times* were in complete accord.

The 1928 revised version of the Prayer Book, known as 'the Deposited Book', imposing in particular more restrictive conditions on reservation, was rejected in the Commons by 268 votes to 222, though both in 1927 and in 1928 the revision would have been passed if MPs from English constituencies alone – and it only affected England – had been allowed to vote. In speeches against the bill, Members of Parliament presented the proposed changes as part of a conspiracy to return England to the Roman obedience, and to that end the Malines conversations were cited as evidence.[21] But also problematic from the perspective of the more Protestant MPs was the absence of penalties being laid down for contravention of the rubrics. The bishops had agreed among themselves to act together in enforcing the rubrics, but as one of the motivating forces behind the revision was the wish to restore discipline within the Church of

---

19 A point made by Maiden, *National Religion*, p. 38. He adds that the revision 'rejected the Ultramontane exoticisms and baroque excesses of continental Catholicism' (p. 41), practices which appealed to League members.

20 Quoted Palmer, *Gadfly for God*, p. 164. Writing anonymously, the paper's editor at the time, Sydney Dark, remarked of the Prayer Book controversy, 'It was the editor's task to keep his paper on the fence without letting his readers realize that it was there at all; and it can be said that this acrobatic feat was performed with almost complete success' (quoted Palmer, *Gadfly for God*, p. 163).

21 Maiden, *National Religion*, p. 151.

England on matters such as reservation and Benediction, this seemed a very weak compromise.[22]

The Sodality of the Precious Blood had its own take on the situation. They issued a statement, quoted in a brief history of the Sodality, which appeared in the February 1990 issue of *The Messenger*, written by the then Priest Director of the Sodality, Fr Graeme Rowlands:

> No such ordering by authority can be acceptable while order in more important matters is not enforced: namely the celebration of Mass in every Parish Church and Cathedral every Sunday and Holy Day of obligation, the use of canonical vestments in every church, the cessation of the celebration by Bishops in their walking attire, the abolition of Evening Communion, and of open encouragement by Bishops of the ministration of Holy Communion to Schismatics.

The Messenger naturally greeted with delight the failure of the bishops to carry their 1927 bill through the House of Commons: 'The proposed new Prayer Book has been Deposited in its proper place, the lumber room. For this deliverance from a menace we are devoutly thankful, although it has been wrought by strange and humiliating means. A purely secular House of Commons largely composed of unbelievers and schismatics, wholly incompetent for theological or liturgical judgment, and swayed by an unintelligent Protestantism, has refused to give legal sanction to the Forms accepted by Convocation.' And it added, 'Let us adopt these points on which to rally: *"No revision until the methods of appointment of Bishops is amended." "No revision until the majority of the present Bench of Bishops has been replaced by others properly elected by the Church."*'[23]

Even the Church Unity Octave was brought into the debate.

---

22 For more details of the proposed revision, see G. J. Cuming, *A History of the Anglican Liturgy*, 2nd edition (London: Macmillan, 1982), pp. 165–90.

23 *The Messenger*, January/March 1928, italics in the original. The notice recognized there might be another attempt to pass the Book by 'diluting the truth to suit the British palate' – as indeed there was later that year.

In the same issue of *The Messenger* which has just been quoted, there was an appeal to members to observe the Octave, and the piece went on: 'The recent exhibition of the Church's subservience to the State and the indiscipline of the Bishops make it increasingly obvious that the remedy can only be found in an external authority, or rather in return to that natural obedience to the authority of the Whole Body centred in the Holy See.'[24] This was, of course, the stated purpose of the Catholic League and it was also the original aim of the Octave of Prayer for Church Unity.

The Octave was first mentioned in *The Messenger* in the October/December issue of 1916, where it was explained what has just been said, that the purpose of the Octave was also that of the League, the 'restoration of the unity of the Catholic Church'. The writer went on to say that it had been granted an indulgence by Pope Benedict XV in a brief commending its observance to the whole Church. The Octave, it was remarked, 'first became widely kept in America'.[25] In fact it had been an Anglo-American initiative ultimately arising from Spencer Jones's book *England and the Holy See*,[26] whose publication aroused great interest and much correspondence from around the world. One of those to write to Jones was the American Episcopal priest Lewis Thomas Wattson. In 1898 he had founded the Friars of the Atonement at Graymoor in New York State as a Congregation in the Franciscan family to work for Christian unity. When becoming a member of a religious Congregation he took, as was customary, a new name, Paul James Francis – though he was more commonly known simply as Fr Paul. Wattson and Jones continued to exchange letters, becoming close friends, and in the course of one exchange in November 1907 Jones suggested that the feast of St Peter on 29 June would be a particularly appropriate day to preach and to pray for the unity of the Church. Wattson, however, suggested that a better date would be the feast of the Chair of St Peter, on 18 January, and as a consequence the Octave of Prayer for

24 Ibid.
25 Ibid., October/December 1916.
26 See above, p. 4n8.

Christian Unity, first celebrated in 1908, took place between the Feast of St Peter's Chair and the Feast of the Conversion of St Paul on the 25 January. In 1909 the firmly papalist community at Graymoor entered the Roman Communion en bloc, an event which served to make the Octave better known, especially among Roman Catholics. It received a further boost by being given papal approval in 1909 and, as mentioned above, was granted an indulgence in 1916.[27]

The Catholic League undertook to foster the Unity Octave, and in 1925 a Council for Promoting Catholic Unity was formed out of present and former members of the League's own Council, under the chairmanship of Henry Joy Fynes Clinton, to spread the observance of the Octave. A report of the work of the Council estimated that, in 1935, some 1,500 clergy were keeping the Octave and, it added, that the number of clergy agreeing with its dogmatic basis was 942, up from 72 in 1929. It was announced in 1936 that yet another society would be formed 'with the one and simple aim of accomplishing on the basis of full dogmatic agreement, a complete reunion, under her hierarchy of the Anglican Communion with the Holy See'.[28] It was to have its own distinctive Catholic hymnal containing popular hymns to the Blessed Sacrament and to Our Lady, together with hymns from the (Roman Catholic) Divine Office. There would be about 200 hymns in total, and the book would sell for 8d., or 6d. each, if 50 copies were to be ordered.[29]

After a number of high-profile conversions to their faith, Roman Catholics might well have expected what the Catholic League was apparently promising to deliver. A correspondent for the RC weekly *The Tablet* reported on a quarterly meeting of 'the Papal wing of the Anglo-Catholics in Caxton Hall', London, in October 1936. The report was republished verbatim in the *Church Times* for 30 October. 'On the platform a committee of Anglican clergymen, birettaed and soutaned', wrote

---

27 See Yelton, *Anglican Papalism*, pp. 25–6.

28 A circular letter from Fynes Clinton in March 1936 announcing the establishment of this society is printed in Salter, *The Anglican Papalist*, pp. 178–9.

29 *The Messenger*, May/September 1936.

the RC observer, 'telling a hall full of Anglicans that "we are in schism, and the sooner it is ended, the better"; that "we are committed to the acceptance of the Holy Father as the divinely-appointed centre of Catholic unity"; that "fidelity to the Faith in its entirety is the greatest glory of the Papacy"; that "one thing the Popes have always done is to teach the fullness of doctrine; they have never compromised with heresy; they will not compromise about that now. If we seek reunion with Rome, we must have the Pope with his doctrine, for that and that only is Rome." And as those hundreds of Anglicans punctuated every reference to the Pope with applause.'

The reporter had his doubts:

Was this reunion business not a pretence, a piece of mimicry, a parade, a Utopia, a pretext to evade individual conversions? There being something wrong somewhere, I sought an interview after the meeting with one of the clerical leaders, a charming old man whose saintly smile was encouragement enough for the most impudent questions: 'What is the size of this movement,' I asked. 'We are exactly 1,016 clergymen,'[30] he replied, 'who have, these last eight years subscribed to the faith of the Council of Trent, and pledged ourselves to preach it to our parishes. Moreover, some two thousand others are in sympathy with our aims, and join us every year with their parishioners in a Novena for the return of the Anglican Church to the Papacy.' 'But is this not discouraging individual reconciliations?' 'We rather encourage them if they are prompted by God's grace. Besides, their number is negligible in comparison with the extent of this movement.'

This account, headed 'Reunion', occasioned a considerable correspondence in which the Catholic League was forced to defend itself. On 13 November, the *Church Times* published a letter from one of the League's founders, R. W. Langford James, in which he wrote:

---

30 'We should very much like to have the names of the 1,158 priests who are marching where Mr. Fynes Clinton leads,' said the *Church Times* on 29 January 1937.

It has recently been my good fortune to hear an address from a Roman priest who is sympathetic towards reunion. He has a double doctorate, and is, therefore, out of the ordinary run. He declared, from his own intimate knowledge of the Roman Communion, that there are two 'schools of thought' in a region in which many fondly imagine such things do not exist. The one school of thought – to which Manning belonged – is intransigeant [sic], rigid, desirous of multiplying dogmas, keen on an excessive centralization (which the aeroplane, telegraph, telephone, and other modern means of rapid transport render only too easy), and zealous for modern cults of saints and the development of such devotions as Benediction. The other school – that of Newman and Mercier – is more charitable, deprecates the tightening up of dogma, regards the Church as more of a federation of local Churches grouped round a common centre in Rome, and clings to the older devotion with Mass and Office as its norm. It is in this latter school that the hopes of reunion are to be placed. It is, this priest averred, more numerous than the other, but at present the other is more powerful, as it has managed to capture the key positions.

It was a statement more perhaps about the hopes of members of the League than a description of 1930s' Roman Catholicism.

Despite frequent efforts by the editor ('This correspondence must cease'), there was a long exchange of letters in which no less a figure than H. L. Goudge, Oxford University's Regius Professor of Divinity, joined with not only an impressive display of logic but also demonstrating a clear understanding of the position of Roman Catholicism. Athelstan Riley, the last Master of APUC, also contributed. There had been another meeting at Caxton Hall, addressed by, among others, Fynes Clinton and Spencer Jones. It was Spencer Jones whom Riley directly addressed: 'It has been widely spread that thousands of Anglican clergy are pledged to the recognition of the modern Petrine claims; may I plead with him to take steps to prevent such a flagrant misrepresentation, and may I suggest that intending intercessionists should be protected from such misconstruction? Nothing could do more harm to the Catholic cause in the country than the suspicion that our clergy are not "straight"; not by such methods can the wounds of Christendom be healed.'[31]

Although the Catholic League continued to advertise its events in the pages of the *Church Times*, the editor's hostility to the papalist position adopted by the League and vigorously defended in its letter columns, continued unabated. *The Messenger* editorialized that there was 'need for a Catholic paper'.[32] The *Church Times*'s disinclination to accept the League's stance, however, was not in the view of the League's members its only failing. It was also at fault for not displaying uncritical support for the Nationalist cause in the Spanish Civil War. This, the League appeared to think, was the *sine qua non* of a valid claim to the title of 'Catholic', for it was the stance of all the British Roman Catholic press with the honourable exception of the Dominican magazine *Blackfriars*.[33] The Octave of Prayer for Christian Unity, on the other hand, was a cause on which all Catholics could agree, as long as the League's strongly papalist position was not to the fore. But then, quite unexpectedly, the Octave itself gave rise to problems.

In September 1937 the Abbé Paul Couturier arrived in London to be met by Fynes Clinton and two other Anglican priests with papalist convictions. For several years there had been an exchange of correspondence between members of the League and various priests in France, Belgium and Italy, the Abbé Couturier among them. Couturier, though brought up in Algeria, was a priest of the Archdiocese of Lyons, ordained in 1906. His interest in ecumenism was first sparked by working with Russian refugees and he later spent some time at the Priory of Amay-sur-Meuse, founded by Dom Lambert Beauduin, to further Roman Catholic–Orthodox relations,[34] where he became an oblate. There he also encountered the

---

31 *Church Times*, 1 January 1937.

32 *The Messenger*, May/September 1938.

33 *Blackfriars* published regular surveys of the Roman Catholic press, which was, as has been noted, wholly behind the armies of General Franco.

34 Cf. above, p. 35.

work for Roman Catholic–Anglican unity of Cardinal Mercier and the Malines conversations. In 1936 Fynes Clinton, accompanied by Dom Gregory Dix, the liturgical scholar and monk of the papalist monastery of Nashdom, Anglicanism's primary Benedictine abbey, set off for Lyons where they met the Abbé and others interested in ecumenism. Members of the League were convinced, and no doubt with reason, that their stance on corporate reunion, one that would entail dismantling the current structure of the Roman Catholic Church in Britain, would be more readily received by clergy on the Continent of Europe than by those of their own country.

Couturier's return visit was orchestrated by Fynes Clinton who in London introduced him to sympathetic clergy, including the now very aged Spencer Jones, and then, accompanied by a translator – sometimes Fynes Clinton himself as Couturier did not speak English – sent him on a tour of papalist Anglican institutions including Nashdom and sundry convents.[35] He returned again in 1938,[36] this time calling on people and places who were less pro-papal, and meeting William Temple, then Archbishop of York but in 1942 to become Archbishop of Canterbury. He was frequently accompanied by Fynes Clinton and other members of the Catholic League, but there was some concern among League members that he was at risk of consorting with Anglican clergy who did not share the League's papalist views.

They had reason for their concern. In 1933 Couturier had already established in Lyon a Triduum of Prayer for Christian Unity, which, after his experiences in England, he transformed into a Universal Week of Prayer for Christian Unity, sharing the same dates – from the Chair of St Peter to the conversion of St Paul – as the League-sponsored Octave. It was this Week of Prayer, with a much wider appeal than the Unity Octave, which gained ground in Britain to the detriment of the Fynes Clinton-backed version, but Fynes continued to support the papalist Church Unity Octave until the end of his life – he died

---

35 Curtis, *Paul Couturier*, pp. 175–86.
36 Ibid, pp. 197–208. Geoffrey Curtis accompanied Couturier on some of this journey.

in December 1959. There was 'a gradual fading away of the Church Unity Octave', wrote Brooke Lunn. 'I remember it well – each year a decreasing number, very small, meeting under the guidance of Fr Fynes and Fr Ivan Young. The latter had a disconcerting habit, when chairing the meeting, of going off to sleep, which was all right until he woke up, always with a start.'[37]

37 Brooke Lunn, 'Couturier and the Church Unity Octave – from the Anglo-Papalists to the Present Day', in a special edition of *The Messenger* for October 2003/February 2004, entitled *The Unity of Christians: The Vision of Paul Couturier*, p. 30 (available online at https://abbepaulcouturier.blogspot.com/p/the-unity-of-christians-vision-of-paul.html).

4

The Second World War and Its Aftermath

There were battles for the Catholic League to fight on many different fronts during the 1930s. The first was that against contraception. The 1930 Lambeth Conference approved in resolution 15 of contraception 'in those cases where there is such a clearly felt moral obligation to limit or avoid parenthood, and where there is a morally sound reason for avoiding complete abstinence', thus reversing the teaching of earlier gatherings of the world's Anglican bishops. The decision to do so was not taken lightly, and it was the only resolution of the Conference where a vote was taken: there were 193 for it, 67 against and 47 abstaining.

As Cardinal Bourne remarked in a sermon delivered in Swansea, the vote had indeed caused surprise and – he added – scandal around the world. 'The prelates who adopted this resolution', the cardinal thundered, 'have abdicated any claim which they may have been thought to possess to be authorized exponents of Christian morality.'[1] The *Church Times* conceded, 'It is impossible to ignore the very disquieting fact that the Lambeth Conference Resolution 15 has sharply divided the Anglo-Catholic party on a fundamental issue.'[2] That division was not evident in the ranks of the League, whose members resolutely lined up behind the Roman Catholic cardinal and condemned their own bishops. And not only on contraception.

---

1 Quoted, from *The Times* in *The Messenger*, October/December 1930. Pope Pius XI responded with an encyclical on Christian marriage, *Casti Connubii*, dated 31 December 1931.

2 *Church Times*, 5 December 1930, p. 722.

They likewise rejected the statement that the Anglican Communion 'repudiate[s] any idea of central authority other than the Council of Bishops', which would, in their view, lead to 'divergence to the point even of disruption'. The bishops at Lambeth had expressed the belief that this would not happen because of the guidance of the Holy Spirit. But, said *The Messenger*, the Holy Spirit had already established in papal authority a means of holding the Church together.[3]

A critic might have responded that the League's position on theology and the liturgy amounted to 'divergence to the point even of disruption'. The League's members, however, continued to argue that the Church of England was fully a part of the Roman Communion though forcibly parted from Rome by Henry VIII. They traced their ancestry as a movement within the C of E to John Keble's Assize Sermon on 14 July 1833, entitled 'National Apostasy'.[4] They were, they believed, in direct line of succession to the Tractarians and produced their own set of tracts – the Oxford Centenary Tractates – to prove it. They expressed great anxiety 'in the efforts of some prominent Anglo-Catholics, supported by the *Church Times*, to manufacture and nourish a special insular, British, "non-papal" form of Christianity ... Anglo-Catholics are seizing the opportunity of the Centenary to pass off Anglicanism as a true Catholicism.'[5]

Pope Pius XI announced a Holy Year for 1933 to celebrate the (presumed) 1900th anniversary of Christ's death. The League 'rejoiced at the inspiration of the Holy Father' in proclaiming a Holy Year and organized a pilgrimage to Rome, taking in on the way a visit to the Holy Shroud of Turin, 'borne by the Archbishop and six Bishops in a great frame, and the marks were perfectly visible at a considerable distance'. The small group of eight priests 'and some lay people' led by Fynes Clinton then went on to Rome, where they visited the traditional sites and

3 *The Messenger*, January/March 1931.

4 *Keble's Assize Sermon: Centenary Edition* (London and Oxford: A. R. Mowbray, 1931). 'The sermon here reprinted is one of the most famous ever preached in the English Church', says the 'Introductory Note'.

5 *The Messenger*, July/December 1932.

had an audience with Pius XI – some, Fynes among them, being physically closer to the Pope than others – and were able to hand over a copy of the Oxford Centenary Tractates, 'bound in tooled morocco'. The papal audience was facilitated by Bishop Michel d'Herbigny SJ. The account of this pilgrimage in *The Messenger*[6] describes d'Herbigny as 'a good friend of the cause of Reunion'. Later that year d'Herbigny, who had been born in Lille, was suddenly exiled from Rome to Belgium and in 1937 stripped of his episcopal privileges and packed off to a Jesuit noviceship in France. There he spent the rest of his life, dying 20 years later without the reason for his sudden disgrace ever being made public. Before this, however, he had enjoyed close connection with members of the Catholic League through a shared interest with many League members, and especially with Fynes Clinton, in the Eastern Churches – from 1922 he was in charge of the Pontifical Oriental Institute.[7]

As has been seen above, the 1930 Lambeth Conference caused particular anguish to League members, and indeed other Anglo-Catholics, with its stance on birth control as expressed in Resolution 15. Resolution 40, however, caused just as much consternation, and for far longer. Section (b) stated:

> The Conference notes with warm sympathy that the project embodied in the Proposed Scheme for Church Union in South India is not the formation of any fresh Church or province of the Anglican Communion under new conditions, but seeks to bring together the distinctive elements of different Christian Communions, on a basis of sound doctrine and episcopal

---

6 Ibid., January/March 1934. There is more on this mysterious character in 'Paul Couturier and the Monastery of Amay-Chevetogne' by Dom Thaddée Barnas, published in a special edition of *The Messenger* for October 2003/February 2004, pp. 96–108, entitled *The Unity of Christians: The Vision of Paul Couturier* (available online at https://abbepaulcouturier. blogspot.com/p/the-unity-of-christians-vision-of-paul.html).

7 According to John Pollard's *The Papacy in the Age of Totalitarianism* (Oxford: Oxford University Press, 2014), p. 182, d'Herbigny was opposed to Lambert Beauduin's 'softly, softly' approach to the Eastern Churches not in communion with Rome, and was largely responsible for the Benedictine's exile from his own foundation at Amay (later at Chevetogne).

order, in a distinctive province of the Universal Church, in such a way as to give the Indian expression of the spirit, the thought and the life of the Church Universal.

The next section of the Resolution went on to note 'that a complete agreement between the uniting Churches on certain points of doctrine and practice is not expected to be reached before the inauguration of the union; but the promoters of the scheme believe that unity will be reached gradually and more securely by the interaction of the different elements of the united Church upon one another'.

The problem for the League was the ecclesiological complexion of some of the 'uniting Churches'. What was being proposed, as Resolution 40 (a) put it, was a union of the (Anglican) 'Church of India, Burma and Ceylon, the South India United Church and the Wesleyan Methodist Church of South India'. It was not, however, quite so straightforward because the South India United Church was itself a union of the Congregational and Presbyterian Churches. In the view of the Catholic League, this was a Protestant federation with no claim to valid sacraments or Eucharist. As *The Messenger* for May/September 1936 put it, 'The campaign for the betrayal of the fundamental principles of the English Church is being pressed assiduously in Protestant quarters. It is revealed alarmingly in the scheme for handing over our fellow Churchmen including larger numbers of half instructed Christian natives to the proposed South India Church in which the principle of the Divine Commission of the Priesthood and Apostolic Succession and the authority of the Church to teach the whole Catholic Faith are jettisoned.'

It had been agreed in 1928 that the Churches would unite under the aegis of the Lambeth Quadrilateral,[8] which required

---

8 The Lambeth Quadrilateral, agreed at the Lambeth Conference of 1888, lists the four points that have to be met by any Church wishing to unite with any Church of the Anglican Communion. They are acceptance of (1) the Old and New Testaments, (2) the Apostles' Creed as the baptismal symbol, (3) the two sacraments of Baptism and the Lord's Supper, and (4) the historic episcopate.

the establishment of the episcopate in Churches that had hitherto had a very different polity. But the agreement reached entailed the recognition of the orders of all already existing clergy in the uniting communions, regardless of whether or not they had been ordained by the episcopal laying on of hands. However, episcopal ordination was to be the pattern of commissioning for all future clergy of the Church of South India. It took the uniting Churches a long time to agree to the terms – the Methodists in 1941, the four Anglican dioceses involved in 1945 and South Indian Church not until 1946, allowing the Church of South India formally to come into existence in September 1947. This long-drawn-out process frequently gave rise to protests in the pages of *The Messenger*, as will be seen in later pages.

The death in February 1939 of Pope Pius XI gave the League another opportunity to assert its papalist credentials. On 20 February, ten days after the Pope's death, a requiem Mass was celebrated at St Magnus the Martyr. In his sermon, Fr A. H. Baverstock wrote that the notion of Roman primacy was gaining ground despite the destructive criticism of papal claims, adding that the 'existence of a *Pontifex Major* on the throne of Canterbury is logically consistent with the recognition of a greater throne and a *Pontifex Maximus*'. *The Messenger* quoted from a letter of the late Lord Halifax – he had died in 1934 after a remarkably long life in the service of better relations between the Church of England and the Church of Rome – to defend the League against charges made by 'the *Church Times* and others' that it had differed from Halifax over the role of the papacy. In a letter dated 22 August 1929, Halifax had written, 'I am never able to understand why the acknowledgement of the Pope as the centre of unity, the head of the Church jure divino, and the jurisdiction belonging to the Holy See (all of which have to be accepted if reunion is to be accomplished), necessarily involve the denial of everything else.'[9]

The Catholic League's claim was somewhat disingenuous. Lord Halifax's remarks might be understood in several ways,

---

9 *The Messenger*, May/September 1939.

differing from the interpretation favoured by the League itself. But by the time that particular issue of the League's magazine was in circulation, the Second World War had broken out and there were other, more pressing, concerns to occupy the members of the League.

The Second World War, like the First, was greeted in the pages of *The Messenger* as a 'Crusade for Christian Civilization', and Cardinal Hinsley, the deeply patriotic Archbishop of Westminster, was quoted: 'In spite of the sadness of our times I am full of hope and confidence, for God has, in His mercy, spared us from being allied by the avowed enemies of God in Soviet Russia. Our country has been chosen by God to be on His side, for we are fighting the cause of God and of Truth.'[10] The USSR had, of course, signed a non-aggression pact with Germany a week before the outbreak of war which, two years later, Hitler reneged upon by invading Russia. Thus, much to the discomfiture of Hinsley, the United Kingdom and the Soviet Union found themselves to be on the same side.[11]

The League was in a quandary. It had vociferously defended Franco's Nationalist forces and now discovered that many in Spain were sympathetic to the Nazi regime. The same was true of the supposedly Catholic regime in Vichy France and, of course, of Catholic Italy, now allied to Germany. *The Messenger*, which in its November 1940 to May 1941 issue printed Pope Pius XII's 'Five Peace Points', counterattacked by warning that on the other hand the 'friendliness and hopes of collaboration with the abominable anti-God State of Russia on the part of so many in England equally and rightly cause distrust among Catholics abroad'. The editor then went on to take to task the *Church Times*, 'whose editorship we must deeply regret, since it is calculated irresponsibly to deepen antagonism between Christian Churches at the very moment when all should be done to promote cooperation in many fields continues, week by week its bitter and ignorant attacks on the

---

10 Ibid., May/September 1940.

11 His discomfiture grew when he was approached by the Foreign Office, which was afraid Franco's Spain might join a 'crusade' against the USSR, to speak in favour of the Soviet Union.

Papacy and the Vatican for not hoisting the Union Jack over St Peter's'.[12]

The editor in question was presumably the inimitable Sidney Dark – 'presumably' because in February 1941 he was fired (though he remained in charge until the end of the following month), ostensibly on financial grounds, but in reality because the paper's proprietor was finding him too difficult and opinionated. Among his opinions was the conviction that Pope Pius XI should have done more to restrain Mussolini from invading Abyssinia.[13] On the death of Pius he wrote, 'the greater the influence, the greater is the responsibility, and the future historian, unhappily, will not be able to avoid the conclusion that the impotence of Christendom is largely due to the policy of Rome, its alliance with Fascism, and its failure to realize at the beginning the spiritual significance of Nazi-ism. When the church bells of Vienna pealed out a welcome to Herr Hitler, they were ringing something very like a knell.'[14]

After the election of Pius XII, he wrote an interesting and perceptive piece, worth quoting at length, which might indeed be seen as critical of the papacy, but it also demonstrated that he was aware of the restraints on the Holy See:

It is well for English Catholics to have in mind, at the beginning of another Papal reign, the limitations imposed on Papal authority by political circumstances. The Roman Church is international in its membership and its influence, but it is still intensely national in its supreme direction. Nothing in Italy is more evidently and essentially Italian than the Vatican, its personnel, its atmosphere, its outlook, its limitations. The recent treatment of Mr. Alfred Noyes[15] is sufficient proof of this assertion. Had it been possible to elect an American Pope, the whole course of future history might have been

---

12 *The Messenger*, November 1940/May 1941.

13 Palmer, *Gadfly for God*, p. 169.

14 *Church Times*, 10 February 1939.

15 Noyes (1880–1958) published a biography of Voltaire, the second edition of which ran into difficulties with the Vatican. Hinsley got the ban lifted.

affected. That was never possible. The Pope is Pope because he is Bishop of Rome, and the Bishop of Rome must be an Italian,[16] with Italian sympathies, as Cardinal Hinsley has English sympathies and the American Cardinals American Sympathies. It has always been our view that the Lateran Treaty gave much more to Signor Mussolini than it gave to the Holy See. But the Church had certain Substantial benefits. In addition to the doubtful advantage of a tiny territorial independence, the Church has had both in Italy and in the Near East such considerable returns from the Treaty that any actual breach with the Fascist government is extremely unlikely. So long as this association continues, and it is difficult to see how it can be broken, a tremendous responsibility rests on non-Roman Catholics, and particularly on the Anglican Communion, to recognize that the struggle of ideologies is the war of Christ against anti-Christ, that the claim of the State to control the individual soul is one to which civilized Christendom can never surrender its hard-won Spiritual independence. It is within the competence of His Holiness the Pope to call the whole Christian world to a holy war, a war fought with prayer and faith to save the world from spiritual thralldom and material destruction. No other man has his authority. Considering the incalculable difficulties, it will not be surprising if the call is not broadcast from the Vatican, and it will not be for lesser men to criticize or condemn.[17]

Dark was succeeded by the theologian and patristic scholar George Leonard Prestige, who had served as deputy editor. Prestige wrote in his editorial for 2 January 1942: 'Side by side with this interest in Christian sociology and its practical application, has gone a unifying movement among Christians of different allegiances. The Roman Catholic Sword of the Spirit Movement has been the most striking example, and the inspirer

---

16 Pope John Paul II, elected in 1978, was the first non-Italian Bishop of Rome since Hadrian VI, who died in 1523.

17 *Church Times*, 10 March 1939.

of impressive demonstrations, in London and provincial centres, in which Churchmen and Nonconformists have participated. The future success or failure of the movement, which has aroused much sympathy and good will, must depend largely on whether its Roman Catholic leaders can bring themselves to work on equal terms with non-papal Christians.'

It transpired that, with a few distinguished exceptions, RC leaders could not in the end bring themselves to work alongside 'non-papal' Christians. Although the Sword flourished, Cardinal Hinsley's original intention of creating a single dynamic organization to bring the Churches behind the war effort was frustrated. Nonetheless, Prestige continued for several years to report on the Sword's doings up and down the country. In the pages of the Catholic League's *Messenger,* however, there was not a single mention of this significant ecumenical initiative by the Archbishop of Westminster.[18]

The war curtailed the League's activities, especially pilgrimages, and the church of St Magnus the Martyr was so badly damaged in a bombing raid on the night of 8 September 1940 that it could no longer be used: services were transferred to the chapel in the crypt.[19] Moreover, wartime paper shortages reduced the League's journal to a six-monthly publication, much of which was concerned with conflicts, as it saw them, within the Church of England. In its June to November issue for 1942 it accused the Bishop of London, Geoffrey Fisher, of taking advantage of the nation's absorption in the war with Germany 'to entrench episcopal autocracy by centralising finance and control in a socialist bureaucracy'. There was, too, an implied attack on the Malvern Conference of 7–10 January 1941, which had been held in Malvern School. The conference was described by Cyril Garbett, then Bishop of Winchester who was later to become Archbishop of York, as 'a gathering

---

18 For the Sword of the Spirit, see Michael Walsh, *From Sword to Ploughshare* (London: CIIR, 1980), and my two-part article, 'Ecumenism in Wartime Britain', *Heythrop Journal* 23 (1982), pp. 234–58, 377–94.

19 Doolan, *The First Fifty Years,* p. 24. The church was reopened on the feast of the Sacred Heart (1 June), 1951, with a blessing from the Bishop of London and in the presence of the Lord Mayor.

of Left Wing intelligentsia',[20] and there were indeed proposals made at the conference to end all private ownership of property and particularly of industry. Among its conclusions were the proposal that the Church of England should reform its own finances and administration, changes that Bishop Fisher was attempting to make in his diocese.

More central to the League's concerns at this time, however, were 'the renewed efforts of some of the Bishops to check Catholic worship and use the hateful 1928 Prayer Book as in the recent "Regulation" for the dioceses of London and Rochester'. There was indeed a revival of interest in, and much discussion of the status of, the 1928 Prayer Book in the early 1940s, largely for the same reason it had been originally introduced: a desire to bring about more discipline in the forms of liturgy approved for churches of the Anglican Communion. It was understandable that League members would see this as a threat to their own preferred manner of worship.

But there was an even greater threat on the horizon. In 1941 the Methodist Church in India voted to join the Church of South India.[21] There was, announced *The Messenger*, a 'Plot for a False Union'. If there was one thing which should arouse clergy and laity alike from their apathy it was the fact that laymen (i.e. ministers who had not been episcopally ordained) 'are to have the right and duty of celebrating Communion', and have equal status in the new Union with those who had been ordained by bishops.[22] The Catholic Advisory Council created the Council for the Defence of Church Principles, under the chairmanship of the Superior General of the Cowley Fathers,[23]

---

20 Quoted by E. R. Norman in *Church and Society in England 1770–1970* (Oxford: Clarendon Press, 1976), p. 366.

21 Cf. above, p. 53f.

22 *The Messenger*, June/November 1943. The same issue recorded the death of Spencer Jones, who, in addition to his ministrations as rector of Moreton-in-the-Marsh, had been President of the Church Unity Octave Council. 'His many works on our relations with Rome are standard', remarked *The Messenger*'s editor.

23 The Society of St John the Evangelist was founded in Cowley, just outside Oxford, in 1866 by Richard Meux Benson (1824–1915) who was at the time vicar of the church of St James in Cowley. In 1868 the headquarters

to coordinate opposition. Opposition, of course, proved fruitless and the inaugural service of the Church of South India was held on 27 September 1947. The League and the Council of the Church Unity Octave protested and sent a letter to the Church of South India saying that they could not enter communion with it. The *Church Times* and the League were for once very much on the same side, G. L. Prestige publishing 'an almost contemptuous news story'.[24]

The war over, the Catholic League tried to pick up again the pieces of its old life. It benefitted substantially from the will of Miss Evelyn Few, its long-serving secretary (she was, apparently, known as 'the faithful Few'[25]), who died in July 1946, leaving the League the residue of her estate, calculated to be worth £8,000.[26] The legacy, however, turned out to be somewhat problematic. Part of the money had been bequeathed to Evelyn Few by her sister with the intention that, on her death, it would go to her family. The will itself was not contested by the family, but it was suggested by them that the League was morally obliged to meet Evelyn's sister's intentions. The

---

('Mother House') moved to Marston Street, to the building now occupied by the Anglican theological college, St Stephen's House. The rule of the Cowley Fathers – who put SSJE after their names – was a mixture of the Benedictine and Jesuit traditions, their spirituality being largely based upon the *Spiritual Exercises* of the Jesuits' founder, St Ignatius Loyola. Fr Longridge SSJE's edition of the *Exercises* was translated into many languages, including Spanish, and circulated worldwide with imprimatur, apparently without many readers realizing he was not a Roman Catholic.

24 Palmer, *Gadfly for God*, p. 205. The newspaper changed its view a couple of years later. For an account of the relations between the Church of South India and the Anglican Communion from the perspective of someone who was, as a Methodist missionary, closely involved, see A. Marcus Ward, *The Pilgrim Church* (London: the Epworth Press, 1953), pp. 36–52. Dr Ward once described himself in the hearing of the present author as 'a very High Church Methodist'.

25 The reference was to a verse in a hymn favoured by Catholic-minded Anglicans, 'Thy hand, O God has guided', with its refrain 'One faith, One Church, One Lord' for which, 'the faithful few fought bravely, to guard the nation's life'.

26 To call her a 'long-serving secretary' is perhaps a little misleading: a founding member, she had served in a number of different secretarial posts, finally as Recording Secretary.

committee sought legal advice, which was, in the end, to reach a compromise with the family. The result was that only half of the money originally destined for the League came to it. Some of her legacy was used to endow a requiem Mass in her memory, a votive candle for Walsingham and to buy a set of vestments for use at Otford during the annual Festa and Corpus Christi procession.[27] These processions began again, though *The Messenger* complained that the practice of members of The Living Rosary of St Dominic wearing a blue mantle for the procession had rather fallen into abeyance. Mantles, members were reminded, could still be purchased for eight shillings.[28]

The war with Germany had done nothing to improve the League's ecumenical spirit. Shortly before the war ended, a group of members were addressed by Mr (later Professor) A. C. F. Beales, the very energetic secretary of the Sword of the Spirit, on the Vatican's policy during the war. He ended by speaking 'of the development in recent years of the encouragement of co-operation between Catholics and others in humanitarian, social, economic and moral efforts. "Impelled by Charity, we invite co-operation ... a duty to form a united front for these things." "A moral obligation that cannot be avoided".'[29] His message was well received – up to a point. Generosity towards those suffering on the Continent of Europe was all very well, but 'we must refuse the specious appeal of our Bishops to give money for the restoration of Protestant heretical "Churches". True charity must prevail over false sentiment. There is no Christian charity in furthering false teaching, the leprosy of souls.'[30]

In the immediate aftermath of the war, the League began to comment on political and social issues of the day rather more readily than it had in the past. Under the headline 'The unjust invasion', Fynes Clinton took the British government to task for 'encouraging the invasion of a friendly country'. While expressing sympathy for the sufferings of the Jewish

27 Doolan, *The First Fifty Years*, p. 26.
28 *The Messenger*, May/October 1949.
29 Ibid., December 1944/June 1945.
30 Ibid., July/December 1945.

people under the Nazi regime, he strongly opposed the return of Jews to Palestine. In what would now be seen as a distinctly fundamentalist reading of the Hebrew Scriptures, he went on 'Some believe that the return of the Jews to the Holy Land is prophesied in the Old Testament; but these prophecies were fulfilled in letter [sic] by the Return from Captivity, in 537 BC'. And he continued, 'Let us do all possible to succour them [i.e. the Jews] and re-establish their lives; but this cannot justly be done by forcing injustice on others' – though there were large numbers of Arabs living in Palestine, he believed that 'the mass of the country people is indigenous and indubitably descendant from the ancient Canaanite tribes which inhabited it centuries before the Israelites were heard of'. *The Messenger* then went on to cite a statement by the Palestine Christian Union, representing all denominations 'in complete agreement, in principle and deed, with their Moslem Brethren', opposing the plan to partition the country.[31]

The Messenger returned to the theme in its May/October 1949 issue: 'A plot has been discovered for the invasion of Yorkshire by a million Jews financed by American dollars and armed by the Communist satellite Czecho-Slovakia, in order to establish a separate state on English soil after evicting from their homes and towns and lands 700,000 of our people to make room for the despoilers.' 'This is not true', readers were reassured in an article headed 'The Rape of the Holy Land', but it was comparable to what was happening in British-controlled Palestine.

In a further foray into politics, the January/July 1948 issue reprinted a statement of the Roman Catholic hierarchy, condemning Communism 'in view of the lack of definite lead from our own [Church of England] Bishops'.

Normal service was, however, swiftly restored as the League reacted to proposals for a celebration to mark the four hundredth anniversary of the 1549 Book of Common Prayer. Opposition was based on the familiar grounds that the BCP had been imposed upon the Church by Parliament, with no

---

31 Ibid., January/July 1948.

canonical authority. 'It is one of the chief causes of division from the rest of the Catholic Church and of endless dissension within the Church of England itself.' In the view of the League, only those service books in use before the break with Rome had any liturgical standing.[32] A later article on the same theme, headed 'The Disaster of 1549',[33] drew attention to the ancient Catholic rites, including the use of chrism in the sacrament of confirmation and prayer for the dead together with the invocation of saints, which had been lost when the BCP became the norm: 'The duty of priests and people is to follow the fathers of the Catholic revival by more and more reviving the use of the ancient service books in public worship.' A pamphlet on the topic by the Revd A. H. Baverstock was promised, priced 5d, post free, or 3/6 per dozen.

Given the hostility of members of the Catholic League towards the role of Parliament as displayed particularly in the Prayer Book revision controversy, it might be expected that the League would be in favour of disestablishing the Church of England and thereby cutting itself free from oversight by the English state. This may have been a long-term goal, but there were voices arguing against such a course of action. Fr Ivan Young pointed out that in Britain conflicts between Church and state had, thankfully been avoided, unlike the situation on the Continent of Europe, something which he put down to the way, in Britain, state and Church had grown organically. 'The purely secular state', he concluded, 'can never regard the Church with a friendly eye.'[34]

The August 1948/April 1949 issue of *The Messenger* contained an announcement of a significant change in the structure of the League. There had long been a Chantry Fund to provide Masses for deceased members.[35] It was decided in 1948 that the endowment of this Fund should be handed over to the Walsingham Trust Association, which was composed of the Guardians of the shrine at Walsingham. Vacancies among

32 Ibid., August 1948/April 1949.
33 Ibid., May/October 1949.
34 Ibid., November 1949/April 1950.
35 See above, p. 29.

the Guardians were filled by co-option so that, members were advised, the Catholic nature of the Trust could be ensured.[36]

Mention of Masses for deceased members is a reminder that while the Catholic League was not itself the major force in the battle for the Catholic tradition within the Church of England – that role was played by the Church Union as a body representing Anglo-Catholic societies in England[37] – the League played a significant role through the Apostleship of Prayer, the Living Rosary and other devotional practices such as retreats and pilgrimages in fostering the spiritual life of its members. *The Messenger*, for instance, gave considerable prominence to the Holy Year announced by Pope Pius XII and which lasted from Christmas 1949 to Christmas 1950, printing the bull of proclamation, *Jubilaeum Maximum*. Fynes Clinton and Ivan Young made a pilgrimage to Rome to mark the Holy Year, together with the League's Secretary, Mr L. G. Fisher. The two priests – Mr Fisher had to return home before the event – were received at Castel Gandolfo by Pope Pius, in an audience (Fynes noted) that lasted 13 minutes. They were, Fynes told the Pope, representatives of the more than 1,400 clergy who were supporters of the Church Unity Octave. Pius blessed the two priests, 'and all your works'.[38]

---

36 Ibid., August 1948/April 1949. See also Doolan, *The First Fifty Years*, p. 27: 'The endowments of the Foundation were transferred to the St John's Prebend for the service of the Catholic League Chapel, and the Chantry masses are now said there by members of the College of priests attached to the shrine.' However, according to an email from the present (12 September 2016) Priest Administrator of the shrine, this is not quite what happened: 'When the Catholic League Chantry Roll was handed to the Shrine it was incorporated into the Shrine's daily cycle of prayer for the departed. The practice here is that those on the Chantry Rolls are prayed for on their anniversary of death at the 7.30am Mass, and continues to be an important element of our work of intercession. "The College of Priests" would refer to "The College" that Fr Patten sought to establish here, and whilst that was one part of his vision that never really established itself it is the Shrine clergy [who] continue to offer the 7.30am Mass each day.'

37 Founded in 1859 as the Church of England Protection Society, it became the English Church Union the following year. After amalgamating with the Anglo-Catholic Congress in 1933, it became the Church Union.

38 It is very difficult to determine how many people were members of the Catholic League at any given moment. While it certainly cannot be pre-

The purpose of the Octave was to make intercession 'specifically for the restoration of corporate reunion of the Anglican Communion with the rock from which we sprang, the Holy See', but, as has already been remarked, there was also a Week of Prayer for Christian Unity,[39] scheduled for the same period of the Church's year, with a rather wider aim. *The Messenger* dwelt upon this distinction between the Octave and the Week, but also took the opportunity to attack once again the proposals for the establishment of the Church of South India. Joint action with other Anglo-Catholic bodies was being contemplated 'and we hope that the council for the Defence of Church Principles and the Church Union will be firm and give a strong lead'.[40] Despite the claim, quoted above, that 1,400 priests celebrated the Octave, it was by the early 1950s in terminal decline. The last call for it to be celebrated was made in 1964, by which time many of the leading Anglican Papalists had died.[41]

sumed that all of the 1,400 priests mentioned in 1950 by Fynes Clinton were members or adhered in their entirety to the doctrinal positions of the Church Unity Octave Council (in fact only 839 did so, cf. *The Messenger* for May to October 1950), in addition to the clergy, the League counted lay people among its subscribers. The November 1949/May 1950 edition of *The Messenger* notes that the Annual Festival for 1949 held as customary at Otford Court had drawn a crowd of about 400, a figure which 'reached quite pre-war dimensions'.

39 Cf. above, p. 49.
40 *The Messenger*, November 1950/May 1951.
41 Yelton, *Anglican Papalism*, p. 61.

1 The Revd Henry Joy Fynes Clinton, effectively the founder of the League, its longest serving priest director and the Rector of St Magnus, London Bridge 1921–59.

2 St Mary's Church, Corringham, Essex.

3 Annual Pilgrimage to Walsingham, 1928 or 1931 (from the archive of the Shrine of Our Lady of Walsingham). Fr Fynes Clinton is seated centre with Father Nicholas Behr, rector of the Russian Orthodox parish in London to his left.

The Catholic League

Anniversary Festival

AT

St. Michael's School

OTFORD COURT, KENT

(By kind invitation of the Rev. T. G. Blofield)

Saturday, 3rd June 1961

(after Corpus Christi)

HIGH MASS - 12.15 p.m.

Solemn Procession of the

BLESSED SACRAMENT

in the Grounds of Otford Court

3.30 p.m.

All Catholics invited

Otford Court is about half-mile from Otford Station on the
Otford-Kemsing Road.   Fifteen minutes walk

Plenty of Parking space for Coaches and Cars

Trains from Victoria 11.15, 2.15   Cheap Day Return fare 8/6

Full particulars 2d. stamp—Gen. Sec., C.L.
L. G. FISHER, 40 Barnmead Road, Beckenham, Kent

4 The annual Corpus Christi Festa, 1961.

5 Annual Festa, Otford Court, 1961. Thurifer: Geoffrey Wright, General Secretary 1975–2002.

6 At a commemoration of the Protestant Reformation Martyrs at Smithfield, League members hold a silent witness in reparation for the persecution of Catholics during the Reformation. Late 1960s. Second from left: the Revd A. T. John Salter, biographer of Fynes Clinton.

7 Diamond Jubilee, Corringham, 1973. Crucifer: David Chapman, General Secretary, 2002.

8 Melkite Divine Liturgy at the Begijnhof Church on the League's annual pilgrimage to Bruges, 2010, celebrated by Archpriest John Salter.

9 Walsingham, 2003. Procession from the Anglican Shrine to the
Dower House for the dedication of the Martyr's Cell as a place
of prayer for unity, reconciliation and reparation for the harm of
disunity. Thurifer: The Revd Christopher Stephenson, priest director
of the Apostolate of Prayer, 2008. Third from right, the future Bishop
Norman Banks of Richborough; sixth from right, the future Bishop
Philip North of Burnley.

10 The Martyr's
Cell, Dower House,
Walsingham, possible
site of imprisonment of
Fr Nicholas Mileham,
last Augustinian sub-
prior of Walsingham
who resisted the
surrender of the
monastery and the
Holy House to Henry
VIII's Commissioners.
The altar was given by
members of the League
in honour of Geoffrey
Wright's tireless work
on pilgrimages to
promote Christian
reconciliation.

11 Mass of rededication of the restored Chapel of the Catholic League and the Sodality of the Precious Blood, and Fynes Clinton Chantry (left), Anglican Shrine of Our Lady of Walsingham, 22 February 2018.

12 Mass of rededication of the Fynes Clinton Chantry, 2018. Principal
Concelebrant, Prebendary Graeme Rowlands, Priest Director of the
Sodality of the Precious Blood 1989–present. Preacher: Fr Mark
Woodruff, Priest Director of the League, 2008.

5

Coming to Terms with Vatican II

The 1950s were something of a watershed for the Catholic League, as they turned out to be for Roman Catholics. The decade started traditionally enough with the formal reopening, on 1 June 1951 – the feast of the Sacred Heart – of Fynes Clinton's church, St Magnus Martyr, which had been, as noted above, very badly damaged, all but the crypt chapel, by German bombs in 1940. The church, which had been such a subject of contention when Fynes Clinton first took over, was now rededicated with a blessing by the Bishop of London, William Wand, in the presence of the Lord Mayor and other worthies. In 1954, the church received 'a precious gift': the Carmelites of Lisieux had long been supporters of the Octave of Prayer for Christian Unity and had several times written to Fynes Clinton. Now they gave to the League a 'primary' relic of St Thérèse of Lisieux, which, it was decided, should stay at St Magnus the Martyr as part of its collection of relics 'as long as this church stays in Catholic hands'.[1]

Members were similarly heartened by changes in the Roman Pontifical, detailing the rites for the ordination of priests and the consecration of bishops in the Roman Catholic communion. 'Points affecting the question of Anglican ordination, which have been asserted by our theologians, have been accepted, and it may be seen that the way has been opened for the consideration of this problem.'[2] Unfortunately that proved far too optimistic.

As did much else. The October/December 1957 issue of *The Messenger* announced the establishment 'of a really Catholic

---

1 *The Messenger*, May/October 1954.
2 Ibid., May/October 1951.

paper. Every Catholic Society in the Church of England will be given adequate publicity, pictures and support. In return we shall expect reciprocity! There will be no rancour; rather, there will be undiluted TRUTH.' Intended to be published monthly, *The Dome* duly appeared in mid-January 1958: Michael Rear, the first Anglican student to study in Rome (September 1963 to Easter 1964) became its Rome correspondent. *The Dome* did not, however, survive the editor's decision a couple of years later to become a Roman Catholic. It was eventually replaced by a newsletter, *Crux*, an initiative of the new Director of the Catholic League, C. R. Beresford, who had succeeded Fynes Clinton on his sudden death – at the age of 84 – on 4 December 1959. 'I do most sincerely hope', he wrote, 'that every single League member feel it a duty (even if not a pleasure) to take in and support *Crux*.'[3] The newsletter was a little more success-ful, and in 1965 metamorphosed into a publishing enterprise, called Crux Press, formally owned by the League, but that, too, was of fairly short duration.

The same issue of the League magazine that announced the establishment of *Crux*, also carried a lengthy and enthusiastic account of the meeting between Archbishop Fisher and Pope John XXIII. But all was not well, as the magazine admitted: 'Two Norfolk strongholds have fallen into the wrong hands – Hindolveston and Gresham. A protestant paper hails the latter as "this great victory over Anglo-Catholic Popery after a 40-year struggle".'

Old-style battles had indeed already re-emerged when the priest-in-charge of a small mission in Carshalton, the Revd R. A. E. Harris, 'an elderly Papalist whose views were so uncom-promising that he had never held a living of his own',[4] was removed from the parish where he had served for over 30 years. He had refused the instructions of the new rector of Carshalton to stop using the Roman missal in his services and was conse-quently ousted by Bishop Mervyn Stockwood. After a lively confrontation between the priest and the bishop, Stockwood,

---

3 Ibid., January/April 1961.
4 Yelton, *Anglican Papalism*, p. 62; cf. also Doolan, *The First Fifty Years*, p. 32.

his archdeacon and two police officers changed the locks on the church door, effectively barring the popular curate. This event, in August 1958, was such a throwback to the past that it was ignored by *The Messenger* and even by the *Church Times*.

Harris must, however, have been heartened by an article in *The Messenger* for November 1955/April 1956 by the Revd Peter Sanderson, arguing that as 'the old Latin Rites of Missal, Breviary and Ritual were never abrogated by any act of the Church itself with full knowledge and consent of what she was doing, [hence] they claim a higher allegiance for us from a spiritual point of view, than does the Prayer Book'.

There were plenty of revivals of old battles. *The Messenger* denounced the 'scandal' when, at a World Council of Churches meeting in Evanston, the Archbishop of Canterbury, Geoffrey Fisher, had taken part in an 'open communion'.[5] Similarly the League's long-standing opposition to the Church of South India rumbled on, though without the support they had been expecting. An appeal was sent to 1,600 bishops and priests of the Church of England as listed in *Crockford's Clerical Directory*, calling upon them to repudiate the resolutions of Convocation concerning the Church of South India. 'The result is very disappointing', confessed *The Messenger*. 'Of those who replied about half expressed their approval of the resolutions and those who signed the repudiation were only 163.' This revealed, the piece went on, 'the terrible apathy, disunion and disloyalty to the Catholic Order in a large part of the clergy'.[6]

Even the coronation of Queen Elizabeth II gave rise to controversy. A note in *The Messenger* pointed out that 'when Parliament asks the Sovereign thus crowned to enact a law that contravenes the Law of God, such as Divorce acts, murder of unborn children etc., it is forcing the breaking of the solemn oath she takes and contradicts the whole significance of the Coronation. Such acts have no spiritual force and do not bind in conscience.'[7] Apart from criticism of the 1930 Lambeth

---

5 *The Messenger*, October/December 1954.
6 Ibid., May/October 1957.
7 Ibid., May/October 1953.

Conference's ruling on birth control,[8] little had appeared in the pages of *The Messenger* on questions of moral theology until the 1950s. The 1958 Conference's stance on divorce, however, again raised the ire of the League. Its Resolution 118 recognized 'that divorce is granted by the secular authority in many lands on grounds which the Church cannot acknowledge, and recognises also that in certain cases where a decree of divorce has been sought and may even have been granted, there may in fact have been no marital bond in the eyes of the Church. It therefore commends for further consideration by the Churches and provinces of the Anglican Communion a procedure for defining marital status, such as already exists in some of its provinces.' In 1954, the League had published a pamphlet explaining why Holy Communion should be refused to those who had divorced. Now the Lambeth resolution 'will allow a Bishop to sanction the giving of Holy Communion to those re-married against the English Church Law, that is, to those who have promised in a registry office to live together in adultery, i.e., to have two wives'.[9]

In 1954 there were fears, which in the end came to nothing, over a possible reform of English Church Law. As an article in *The Messenger* explained, 'We priests take an oath to use no book [in church services] but the Book of Common Prayer, unless another is sanctioned by "lawful authority" ... as the Book of Common Prayer has only been enacted by the authority of Parliament and not enacted (but only *permitted*) by Convocation we are doing not only what is permissible but what, under Church as opposed to State law, is proper.'[10] The fear was that the BCP would be *enacted* by Convocation, thus putting those who adhered to what the piece called 'the ordinary Western canon' as used by St Augustine when he arrived

---

8 See above, p. 51.

9 *The Messenger*, October 1958/February 1959. The resolution does not really envisage anything of the sort. The phrase the Church 'recognises also that in certain cases where a decree of divorce has been sought and may even have been granted, there may in fact have been no marital bond in the eyes of the Church', sounds very like the practice in the marriage tribunals of the Roman Catholic Church.

10 Ibid., May/October 1954, italics in the text.

in Canterbury in 597, 'without the alteration of a word or comma', at odds with Church law as well as state law.

Adherents of this romantic vision of the Roman liturgy were shortly in for a considerable shock. They should have seen it coming. *The Messenger* regularly printed excerpts from papal encyclicals and other Vatican documents. In the November 1949/April 1950 issue there were extracts from the papal encyclical *Mediator Dei*, which presaged what were quite modest changes in the way the Mass was conducted, but the League, like very many Roman Catholics at the time, had made much of the conviction that the liturgy had scarcely ever changed at all. Again, some 18 months later, the journal reported some (very minor) adaptations of the eucharistic fast, and in the January/April issue of 1961 there was a lengthy piece on changes mandated by Rome in the rubrics of the Mass, and in the calendar of saints and the Divine Office. But by this time the Second Vatican Council was under way. Forty-six priests belonging to the Sodality of the Most Precious Blood had sent Pope John XXIII a letter welcoming the Council, and the Director of the Apostleship of Prayer, the Revd P. R. Sanderson, included the success of the Council among the Apostleship's intentions in July 1965, having already prayed in the previous quarter (the committee had decided that *The Messenger* was to be produced quarterly) 'That all mistaken protests against Transubstantiation be removed from Church of England formularies'.[11] Sanderson was not sanguine about the possibilities of reunion between Rome and Canterbury, despite the League's best efforts, which, he appeared to suggest, had not been given due recognition by Rome.[12]

Beresford himself, however, was more hopeful. He remarked on 'the extreme significance of recent statements of the Vatican Council regarding the collegiality of the Bishops with the Pope as the Head. It seems to me that this is a tremendous step forward and may well do much to bring official Anglicanism to a favourable frame of mind for a reappraisal of the Petrine texts and the rightful claims of the Holy Father. It is just possible that

---

11 Ibid., April 1965.
12 Ibid., January/April 1962.

it may turn out – for us – the most significant thing the Council has done.'[13] 'Putting the Council's finding into practice' was among the Apostleship of Prayer's intentions for January 1966.

At this point, in the late 1960s, it seemed that, on the surface at least, the Catholic League was flourishing. There were festivals in almost every part of the country, as well as regular pilgrimages to Walsingham and – now – to the Carmelite priory at Aylesford. But there were problems, stemming in particular from Roman Catholic liturgical developments in the wake of Vatican II. Fr Beresford had died unexpectedly in July 1967 and was replaced by the Revd B. E. Joblin. In the April 1968 issue of *The Messenger*, Joblin wrote:

> Especially important it is that in a situation so fluid, we should refrain from impugning the Catholicity of those who may feel that a particular course of action is right, in spite of our disapproval. Mr Peter Anson, in a somewhat derisive letter to the March edition of the 'Catholic Standard', seems to suggest that the Catholic League is an anachronism. We should certainly give point to such a suggestion if we identify ourselves too closely with some particular phase of modern Roman practice which is likely to be out of date in a year or so's time. Let us, whatever we feel is right, refrain from causing dissension by quarrelling with those who decide to do something different. As for the suggestion that the Catholic League is an anachronism, those who made this accusation should consider the glad acceptance of Vatican II in the official statement of the League's standpoint.

In a letter addressed to members in the same issue, Joblin went on to defend the Catholic League against suggestions that, in the light of Vatican II, all Catholic societies within the Church of England, such as the League, the Confraternity of the Blessed Sacrament, the Society of Mary and the Guild of All Souls should be disbanded. As far as 'our League is concerned',

---

13 Ibid., January 1965. Many Roman Catholics would likewise agree on the importance of the doctrine of collegiality embraced by Vatican II, but talking of collegiality is one thing, achieving it is something else again.

he wrote, 'I would wish to repudiate in your names any idea of submission to this religious "nationalising". The Catholic League stands where it has always stood.' He added:

> I think we could reasonably quote Nehemiah (chapter 6, verse 3) – 'I am doing a great work, so I cannot come down: why should the work cease whilst I leave it and come down to you?' Admittedly Nehemiah was addressing his enemies, but I think we can apply his words in illustration of our attitude as a League to the suggestion of our disbandment. Let us keep together and go on quietly, continuing to uphold the Catholic Faith as in the past, without controversy, if it may be, but in loving devotion to the Sacred Heart.[14]

As *The Messenger* never carried a page for readers' letters, what the members themselves thought is impossible to gauge. They were of course free to write to the Director or members of the committee, as did four League ordinands in the latter part of 1966, accusing it of being, in the light of Vatican II, reactionary. The charge clearly hurt Fr Beresford, still at the time League's Director, not least because he was in the process of attempting a revision of the League's leaflet to bring it into harmony with the Council's teachings. Meanwhile the magazine published each quarter a summary, with commentary, of the major documents of the Council.

In his letter published in July 1969, ostensibly on the proposals for an Anglican–Methodist reunion, of which more below, Joblin made the important point that the former rigidity of worship both in the Church of England and the Church

---

14 Peter F. Anson (1885–1975), referred to by Joblin, had been an Anglican Benedictine on Caldey Island and had, with the majority of that community, been received into the Roman Catholic Church in 1913. He went on to become a prolific author on matters ecclesiastical – and on seafaring. Anglo-Catholics were not the only ones to feel disoriented in the aftermath of Vatican II, so were many Roman Catholics. See for instance my article 'The Conservative Reaction' in Adrian Hastings (ed.), *Modern Catholicism: Vatican II and After* (London: SPCK, 1991), pp. 283–88. Like some members of the League, many conservative RCs were particularly disturbed by the liturgical changes, as the article points out.

of Rome had 'fostered the growth of private devotions with the development of special societies, confraternities and associations ... thanks to Pope John and the 2nd Vatican Council – and to the Ecumenical Movement – the pendulum is swinging back to the idea of communal worship, with a consequent depreciation of private prayer and special objects of devotion hitherto recognised and promoted'. Fynes Clinton's Sodality of the Precious Blood was a case in point as, it was reported, very few members now turned up to its meetings. There was a proposal to disband it. In the end, it survived unchanged.[15]

As Joblin had perceptively remarked, the celebration of the Eucharist had rather relativized the devotions in which Catholic Leaguers had once delighted. However, the structure of the Roman Catholic Eucharist which emerged after Vatican II, the so-called 'missa normativa', did not find favour among many of the League's members – or indeed among many RCs. Despite the criticisms, Joblin remarked, 'we recall the basic principle behind all this – of Catholic obedience. It is distressing to hear of those who formerly gave great weight to Papal authority now impugning it because they do not like what the Holy See enjoins.'[16]

This was almost the last injunction of Fr Joblin to League members. On the grounds of ill health – he had, he wrote, almost lost his voice – he resigned to be replaced as Priest Director by the Revd W. Hum of Leeds who promptly appointed as Assistant Priest Director the London-based Revd Raymond Avent. The change of Director notwithstanding, the same debates rumbled on in the pages of *The Messenger*. It was not just the *missa normativa* that was causing problems because

---

15 There is a brief history of the Sodality in *The Messenger* for February 1990, written by its Priest Director, Graeme Rowlands, to commemorate the seventy-fifth anniversary of its founding. The numbers had declined by the end of the 1960s, Fr Rowlands confirms, through deaths and secession to Rome, but from that nadir it has since grown so that 'the number of members now far exceeds that of any previous generation, with a fair number of young clergy'. The requirements of membership remained the same, priestly celibacy, recitation of the Daily Office, by this time in English. Members were also banned from being Freemasons.

16 *The Messenger*, April 1970.

'hanging over our heads is the horrid "Series 3"', wrote Hum, 'concocted by the [Anglican] Liturgical Commission without any apparent Catholic voice'.[17] There was undoubted confusion. Unlike the traditional practice of the Church of England, Roman Catholics had received Holy Communion under only one species – in the form of bread. The Anglican Papalists had copied this practice, and some had even been rebuked for doing so. Now, however, there was growing tendency among RCs to receive under both kinds. Readers' letters were not, as has been remarked, a regular feature of *The Messenger*, but one from the Revd G. A. C. Whatton was published in the January 1972 issue:

> I have been a member of the Priests' Sodality of the Precious Blood for about forty-nine years. I do not however find in myself any reluctance to go along with the Liturgical changes initiated by the authorities of the Western Church as a result of the Constitution on the Sacred Liturgy of the Second Vatican Council. I fail to see why, having all my priestly life followed as a guiding principle the usage of the Western Church, I should suddenly reverse it, and decide against the Liturgical experts of that Church and in favour of the old Roman Rite, which the Council decreed to be in need of revision. Should the habit of years in saying Mass or the Divine Office stand against our general principle? I, for one, think not.

That view was straightforward enough, but as Hum commented in the October 1972 issue of *The Messenger*, not everyone was of a like mind. He expressed regret that, in the upper echelons (as he put it) of the Church of England, in the General Synod and on the Liturgical Commission there were no Catholics. Though the League could claim no particular liturgical competence, he went on, in his view the Western (i.e. Roman) Rite

---

17 Ibid., January 1972. This was, indeed, a departure. There had been 'Catholic voices' on earlier Church of England theological commissions, such as, for example, that of Dr John Moorman, Bishop of Ripon.

most represented the churchmanship of its members. But after the reforms which sprang from Vatican II there was now a variety of rites, and 'it would seem that in differing views on this matter we need to exercise much more charity than at present. It is the Faith which the Liturgy expresses rather than the actual method of expressing it that ultimately counts. It is depressing that those who profess and call themselves Catholic will not worship with other Catholics because of a particular liturgical "use".'

Matters had clearly moved on from what might at this point have seemed the 'fundamentalism' of Fynes Clinton and the early members of the Catholic League. It was a break, occasioned more than anything by the Second Vatican Council, which was perhaps symbolized by a decision of the committee on 5 November 1969 and announced in *The Messenger* for January 1970, to abandon as its profession of faith the creed of the Council of Trent, adopted soon after the League's creation, and use in its place the Credo of the People of God, published by Pope Paul VI on 30 June 1968.[18]

This was not without its complications. Joblin found himself having to explain that the expression 'the fires of Purgatory', which occurred in the Credo, had to be taken metaphorically as no material fire could affect an immaterial soul. More to the point, however, was the Credo's phrase in the section on Church unity, 'the communion of a single hierarchy'. Many, perhaps all, members of the League foresaw reunion in the form of a 'Uniate' Church, such as those of the East, preserving the particular ethos of Anglicanism,[19] and they were encouraged in this by Pope Paul VI's reference to the Anglican Communion as a 'beloved sister' in his homily during the canonization of

---

18 It seems to have been issued as an orthodox response to the controversial Dutch Catechism, which had shortly before been published with the blessing of the bishops of Holland. The outline for the Credo had apparently been drawn up by the 85-year-old philosopher Jacques Maritain (1883–1973), assisted by the Swiss theologian Cardinal Charles Journet (1891–1975).

19 It was in this context that *The Messenger* printed the letter of the Revd E. J. Pizey referred to above, p. 35.

the Forty (Roman Catholic) Martyrs of England and Wales on 25 October 1975. As to the single hierarchy, wrote Joblin, the Pope could not have been intending to leave out the Orthodox Churches and therefore, by extension, he could not have been intending to omit the Anglican Communion either.[20]

---

20 *The Messenger*, January 1970.

6

Old Challenges but New Hopes

The Second Vatican Council and its aftermath, especially the liturgical changes sanctioned by Rome, may not have resulted in the dissolution of the Catholic League, but they certainly caused a fundamental reassessment. In a sermon preached at the League's Northern Festival in Bradford in June 1974, the Revd Kevin Eastell of Toxteth, Liverpool, claimed that 'We have been left "high" and "dry" by the Roman Catholic discipline which has changed dramatically over the past decade since Vatican 2, consequently many specific Anglo Catholic practices have absolutely no authority to substantiate their use from either Roman Catholicism or Anglicanism. Indeed, the reaction to change has meant that many so called "Catholic" parishes have given themselves to a degree of congregationalism and parochialism which, I humbly suggest, is the very antithesis of what we are supposed to represent as Catholics.' The League, he went on, 'exists to promote fellowship amongst Catholics and also to CONVERT [sic] to the Catholic religion. With objects such as these have we any right to ignore the decisions of the Second Vatican Council and thereby strain our fellowship with the larger Catholic witness in the Roman Church? I think not!' Against those resistant to change, he argued that conversion means change: 'For us in the Catholic League we have an immediate function and relevance in bringing to the Anglo Catholic movement that degree of change and flexibility that makes all the difference between the Anglo Catholic movement being part of the Spiritual Renewal or a museum piece.'

Similar sentiments were expressed in the February 1975 issue of *The Messenger* by the Assistant Priest Director Raymond Avent when he announced that the committee had postponed

the appointment of a successor to Fr Hum (in the end, it was
Avent himself who was chosen) while consideration was given
to the future role of the League. Much of what the founders
had fought for had by now been achieved, he argued, claiming
– albeit indirectly – for the League some part in Vatican II. He
did not pause to explain, but went on:

> As Catholics who long for reunion with Rome and who
> work and pray for it, we should be inspired and overjoyed.
> But are we? Have we accepted the spirit of Vatican II or
> are we afraid of the changes it has brought? Are some of us
> perhaps still clinging to our past ideas and ways because we
> cannot accept the inward conversion which renewal always
> demands? Could we be accused of perpetuating a rigidity
> which Rome no longer has? May we be refusing the chal-
> lenge to become more deeply committed Catholics by hiding
> behind past formulas and concepts?

Nothing in the Minutes of the General Committee suggests,
however, that the reflection on the future of the League ever
seriously took place.

Nonetheless, Fr Avent was convinced and set out to convince
others through the pages of *The Messenger* that change was
imperative. Commenting on 'A glorious Eucharist in St Paul's
Cathedral recently, preceded by an all-night vigil and procession of witness [which] brought joy and inspiration to many
Catholics in the home counties', he went on, 'We are moving
out of an era where the emphasis has been on preserving the
status quo, being true to the past, holding fast to what we had.
Perhaps such preservationist attitudes were borne of a need for
consolidation. They resulted in a period when, in our fervent
efforts not to compromise the Faith and to hand it on intact,
we reduced it to a formula, a practice, a ritual. If we are to be
true to our faith we must do more than that. We must hand on
a faith freed from the restrictions of fossilization.'[1]

---

1 *The Messenger*, June 1979. The St Paul's service he mentions took
place on 28 April 1979.

Though the League was eager for unity with Rome – as long as it was corporate reunion – they were thoroughly opposed to proposals for reunion with the Methodists. In this instance it was the Methodist Church which had made the approach to the Church of England in the 1950s, and plans were prepared with remarkable speed. Theologians from the two Churches produced an interim report in 1958, which received the backing both of the Lambeth Conference and of the Methodist Assembly. Five years later *Conversations between the Church of England and the Methodist Church* appeared, outlining a scheme to bring the two bodies into one. The problems that Anglo-Catholics had with the proposals were similar to those which they had perceived in the establishment of the Church of South India, namely the role of bishops and the necessity of ordination by bishops. Many Methodists had their own reservations, again particularly to do with ordination – or, in their case, the proposed re-ordination. They also did not wish to sever their links with the other Free Churches. Opposition to Anglican–Methodist reunion was led by the Society of the Holy Cross rather than by the Catholic League itself, but the Society made every effort to bring on board all the Catholic societies within the C of E. In 1972 the C of E's General Synod rejected the proposals, and members of the League breathed a sigh of relief: 'The final rejection of the lamentable Anglican-Methodist scheme earlier this year', said *The Messenger*, 'is a matter for deep thankfulness.'[2]

When in January 1973 the magazine named three threats, Anglican–Methodist reunion headed the list. The proposals had been defeated, it went on with obvious delight. The second threat was 'the horrid' Series 3, but that might be avoided. The third threat, however, was the ordination of 'priestesses': 'From the other side of the world comes the echo of what John Knox called in another connection the "monstrous regiment

---

2 Ibid., October 1972. This account draws on an article in the May 1964 issue of *The Messenger* by the Revd Arthur Simmons, and on an account by Owen Higgs published in *In This Sign Conquer: A History of the Society of the Holy Cross (Societas Sanctae Crucis) 1855–2005* (London: Bloomsbury, 2007), pp. 160–1.

of women" – the purported ordination of some women to the priesthood, in defiance of all Catholic order and two thousand years of history. We all know that these eccentric episcopal gentlemen can lay hands on the ladies until they are black in the face, but will not confer the sacrament of orders.' The first ordination of a woman – the deaconess Florence Li Tim Oi – had occurred in Hong Kong during the Second World War, to alleviate the shortage of priests, and the practice had been followed in the late 1960s and early 1970s by the Anglican Churches of Canada, New Zealand and the USA.

The line taken by the Catholic League was unequivocal. Some clergy would resign their orders were the ordination of women to be accepted by the Church of England, said the Priest Director in January 1973, and while others would not do so 'we would consider ourselves absolved from any communion with a Bishop who committed such an outrageous breach of Catholic Order. Needless to say, no Catholic worth the name would dream of either attending, still less of receiving, any "communion" purporting to be administered by such female ecclesiastical monstrosities. Again, this crack-brain proposal not only means a great waste of energy and time in combating it, but is also another potential divisive factor at a time when much lip-service is given to "ecumenism".'

Progress in relations between the Anglican Communion and the Roman Catholic Church at that time was deserving of a more positive description than 'lip-service'. At the meeting in 1967 between the Archbishop of Canterbury, Michael Ramsey, and Pope Paul VI it was agreed to establish what became familiarly known as 'ARCIC', the Anglican–Roman Catholic International Commission, whose terms of reference were agreed the following year after a meeting in Malta. The first, or Windsor – named from the place where the discussions took place – Statement appeared in 1971 and was devoted to eucharistic doctrine; the second, or Canterbury, Statement followed in 1973, dealing with ministry and ordination, and the third – the Venice Statement on authority – was published in 1976. There were further meetings, which produced 'Elucidations' of each of these topics, and at a meeting, again at

Windsor, in 1981 there was written a revised version of the document on authority and a Final Report.

The Statements 'are slowly being digested by the two Churches', commented the Revd Barry Keeton,[3] but, he thought, rather more successfully in the Church of England than in the Church of Rome because 'one senses that in the Roman Catholic Church theology is not regarded as the proper province of lay people in general and the impetus to discuss is often lacking ... My impression is that by and large when Roman Catholics discuss them it is usually at the instigation of their Anglican friends.' He added that Continental RCs, in particular the French, seemed more sympathetic to Anglicans than did English ones,[4] possibly, he suggested, because they have had less historical and cultural involvement with the C of E, perhaps because French Protestants are very Protestant and 'Perhaps, too, it would be reasonable to suppose that the spirit of independence from Rome expressed historically in Gallicanism, which was eclipsed during the triumph of ultramontanism, has reasserted itself to some extent as a result of Vatican 2; this would supply another point of contact.' He went on to say – quoting Cardinal Basil Hume's address to the General Synod in February 1978 – that any decision to ordain women would get in the way of further ecumenical progress.

There was no doubt among Anglo-Papalists that the ordination of women would create a major obstacle to reunion with Rome. *The Messenger* in October 1978 published in full a 'Resolution passed unanimously by representatives of Catholic Societies [16 of them] within the Church of England' in which it was argued that such an action could not be taken without the prior agreement of the Old Catholics (with whom, of course, the C of E was in communion), the Roman Catholics and the Orthodox. It would also, the resolution went on, cause 'serious division and disruption' within the C of E itself. And it ended, 'We do not believe that in the foreseeable future, either the ordination of women to the priesthood and episcopate in the

---

3 'Measuring the Momentum', *The Messenger*, July 1978.
4 See Appendix 1 for the attitude of one English RC bishop.

Church of England or the ministration in England of women priests from abroad, would be consonant with the traditional claim of the Church of England to be part of the Catholic and Apostolic Church.'

In September 1979 *The Messenger* reported that the July 1979 General Synod had rejected the proposal that 'women "lawfully" ordained overseas could, in certain circumstances be authorised to celebrate the eucharist here'. There would therefore be, the report observed, another five years before the motion to allow women to minister in England could again be introduced, and it would be a decade before any possible legislation.

League members could relax for now. Whether Roman Catholics would be ready to recognize the Church of England's 'traditional claim', as in the 1978 report, was, apparently, rarely questioned, nor how British RCs might feel about the condescension displayed towards them in Fr Keeton's article just quoted.[5] But in the approach to reunion adopted by the League – at least as recorded in *The Messenger* in the aftermath of Vatican II – the views of RCs in Britain were not significant. The relationship with Rome, the corporate reunion of which Fynes Clinton had so often spoken, was envisaged as a direct link between the Holy See and a 'Uniate' style C of E. This was clearly propounded in an article published in *The Messenger* in January 1976 by Dom Aidan Harker, at the time a monk of Nashdom Abbey, a strongly Anglo-Papalist community.[6] Dom Aidan's argument was that the fact that the C of E was 'not

---

5 The article, as is noted, was published in 1978. Eight years earlier the British Jesuits had moved their college in Oxfordshire, Heythrop, to become part of the University of London, where it played a significant role in the theological education in the Catholic tradition of laity and clergy alike – and not just of Roman Catholics.

6 Nashdom – the word means 'Our House' in Russian – was built between 1908 and 1915 (the exact dates are uncertain) in Burnham, Buckinghamshire, for a Russian prince and princess to a design by Edward Lutyens. In 1924 the house was acquired by an Anglican Benedictine community, which moved there in 1926 and remained until 1987 when the community transferred to Elmore Abbey near Newbury in Berkshire. From 2010 the remaining monks have lived in a house attached to Sarum College, Salisbury.

one outwardly with the rest of the Catholic Church is not all our fault. It is necessary to remember that the Reformation in the sixteenth century might not have taken the course it did but for the sin and neglect of the officials of the Catholic Church.' This is a view which would have been unlikely to resonate with British RCs who were programmed to remember King Henry VIII's desire to divorce Katherine of Aragon rather than to recall Luther's objections to the sale of indulgences or the doctrine of justification by faith alone.[7]

Dom Aidan went on, in a passage which deserves to be quoted at length,

> It is true that English Catholicism has always had certain national characteristics, and, therefore, it is not usual for us to express our thought and devotion in precisely the same way and with the same language as a Spaniard or a southern Italian. But it is not true to say that Church and state are the same thing. For the Catholic religion comes *to*, not *through* a nation; comes to it, as it comes to an individual, to per-fect that which is there, to take all that which is best in the national life and its characteristics and to raise it to a super-natural state. This is what the Pope [Paul VI] meant when, on the occasion of the canonization of the Forty Martyrs of England and Wales [25 October 1970], he said that on the day when the Church of Rome would embrace firmly her ever-beloved Anglican sister in one authentic communion of the family of Christ,

> > No offence will be inflicted on the honour and sovereignty of a great country such as England. There will be no

---

7 When in May 1980 a new minister – at that point the UK and the Holy See did not have full diplomatic relations – presented his credentials to Pope John Paul II as the UK government's representative to the Holy See, he remarked on the improving relations between the Catholic Church and the Church of England. This caused *The Messenger's* editor to comment that the C of E was part of the Catholic Church, and the correct formulation should have been 'between the Apostolic See and the Church of England'. The editor added, 'It is important for diplomatists to get the facts right' (November 1980).

seeking to lessen the prestige and usage proper to the Anglican Church.

This is only one of the imaginative and well-informed gestures which the Holy Father has made towards the Church of England and it is one of great importance. For it implies the recognition of the Church of England as an independent ecclesiastical organization as distinct from the Church organized by Pope Pius IX in 1850.[8]

Where, in this interpretation of events, one cannot but wonder, do those Catholics fit in who remained in communion with Rome from 1540 to 1850?

Dom Aidan found support for at least some of his views in a sermon preached in Cambridge in 1970 during the Week of Prayer for Christian Unity by Cardinal Johannes Willebrands (1909–2006), the President of the Pontifical Council for Promoting Christian Unity, where he spoke of a diversity of theological approaches, and by an article entitled 'United not Absorbed' by Bishop Christopher Butler (1902–86), formerly Abbot of Downside but at this time an auxiliary bishop of Westminster, where he spoke of an '"English Rite", with its own bishops, liturgy and theological tradition'.

He then went on to consider what role the Catholic League might play in the search for unity, now that ARCIC was in full flow. He had a twofold answer. First, by fostering contemporary scholarship and through its publications it might, in conjunction with other Catholic societies, present the faith 'in a way progressively adapted to contemporary understanding' – he is quoting Pope Paul VI; 'Secondly, we must impress upon our fellow Anglicans the fact that as long as the Church of England remains separated from the Holy See, the centre and symbol of unity for all Christians, we are incapable as a Church of exercising the *magisterium* or teaching authority, which belongs to the Church as a whole. Consequently, the Church of England has no power to teach doctrines contrary to

---

8 Pius IX restored a canonically functioning RC hierarchy to England and Wales in 1850.

those defined by the whole Catholic Church.' The logic of the final sentence is something of a puzzle.

There is something of a paradox in citing Cardinal Willebrands because both he and his predecessor as President of the Secretariat for Promoting Christian Unity, Cardinal Augustin Bea SJ (1881–1968), had argued that it would be harmful to ecumenical relations with the Church of England to canonize the Forty Martyrs who had died in the persecution of Catholics in England and Wales during the sixteenth and seventeenth centuries,[9] yet the sermon preached by Paul VI on that occasion obviously gave considerable encouragement to members of the Catholic League, especially with its reference to the C of E as being a 'sister'. The sermon had for the most part been drafted by the two Jesuit postulators (i.e. promotors) of the canonization of the Forty Martyrs, one in Rome, the other at the Jesuit Headquarters at Farm Street, in London's Mayfair. Both were well aware of the sensitivities of Anglicans and had phrased the sermon accordingly. They were likewise almost certainly aware that Bea had promised the Archbishop of Canterbury that the canonization would not happen – a promise which only made the English and Welsh Roman Catholic hierarchy all the more eager to pursue it. But the section which Harker quoted from the sermon, and the reference to the C of E as a 'sister',[10] had not been in the original draft. It had been added by Pope Paul VI himself – and gave rise to much discussion among theologians with an interest in ecumenism.[11]

Dom Aidan's suggestion that the Catholic League should foster research and study was taken up. Together with the Franciscan Friars of the Atonement,[12] ensconced at the time in a friary just south of London's Westminster Cathedral, the League sponsored a series of five public lectures on ecumenism,

9 It perhaps should be explained that, in the Vatican's eyes, England and Wales are one unit, or episcopal conference, Scotland another, and Northern Ireland is part of the Irish episcopal conference.

10 The Pope did not say 'sister Church': was the omission of the word 'Church' deliberate?

11 Cf. Peter Hebblethwaite, *Paul VI: The First Modern Pope* (London: HarperCollins, 1993), pp. 559–61.

12 See above, p. 44.

held in the Westminster Cathedral Conference Centre in October and November 1976. They were, reported the Priest Director, excellent talks and well attended, though 'There was a small but vociferous group of ultra Conservatives who made dialogue difficult at times. Their presence was uncomfortable, but it was salutary to appreciate how much education needs to be done ... The teaching of Vatican 2 is still largely a closed book to most Catholics.' Fr Avent did not specify whether the said Catholics were of the Anglican or the Roman variety.[13] The ultra-conservatives did not, however, discourage the League, again together with the Friars, from sponsoring a day-long conference on 10 February 1979 at the Cathedral Conference Centre on 'A Theology of the Church'; Bishop Christopher Butler was invited to speak on 'A Roman Catholic Approach' and in the afternoon Leslie Houlden of King's College, University of London provided an Anglican perspective.

The turn towards scholarship was continued in the pages of *The Messenger*, which began to carry more learned articles, broke out into colour, at least for the front cover, and began to look more like a regular journal and less like a somewhat scrappy newsletter of the League. One of the first, and perhaps most significant, contributions to the new-style *Messenger* was by Andrew Louth, at the time the chaplain to Worcester College, Oxford, and a patristic scholar. In a piece entitled 'Unity in Diversity', he employed his considerable knowledge of fourth-century Christianity to argue for the possibility of diversity in theology while being united in faith: 'The Church can, and should, accept some pretty wild opinions, so long as they are held as opinions and not held *against* the faith of the Church. Bad theology is better overcome by good theology, not by the methods of ecclesiastical censure' – ecclesiastical censure being at the time the preferred approach of the Church of Rome. He had some critical passages about the Church of Rome,[14] though at the same time acknowledging the pre-eminent

---

13 *The Messenger*, January 1977.

14 Partly perhaps because of a misunderstanding of the – admittedly somewhat arcane – distinction between the Vatican (City) State and the Holy See.

position of the Pope in representing and symbolizing the unity and continuity of the tradition of the Church.

At the centre of his argument, however, was an important criticism of the vision, held by many, perhaps most, in the Catholic League at the time, of the Church of England in future being linked to the papacy through a 'Uniate' structure. The Uniate Churches were those which had at some time in the past been separated from communion with the Church of Rome but which had, again at some time in the past, been reunited with it while maintaining their own forms of the liturgy, including importantly their own liturgical language, and their own canon law, in other words their own traditional culture.[15] Louth pointed out that there had been a cultural convergence between the Church of Rome and that of Canterbury: 'we Anglicans no longer think of the Roman liturgy as a Latin liturgy, but as a part of the variety of English liturgy, in principle (and of course – in the most surprising places too – actually) available to us'. He went on, 'I cannot see the point of uniate status for the Anglicans except as a strictly transitional phase. Certainly in England a uniate Anglican Church would not contribute to the *visible unity* of the Church in this land. But further, the fundamental differences between our communions are not the sort of cultural differences that largely complement one another, differences that should be brought together to fertilize one another and lead to a *new* unity in diversity.'[16]

It would of course take far more than one article to kill off the long-held notion within the Catholic League of a 'Uniate' Church of England, based on a 'patriarchate' of Canterbury. It was a notion propounded even by some Roman Catholic ecumenists. The Revd John Coventry SJ, speaking in Swansea at a meeting of the RC graduate society, the Newman Association, claimed that the creation of new patriarchates in the

---

15 It should be said that the 'Uniate' Churches do not approve of this term, one which is generally regarded by them as derogatory and is often employed by their opponents to belittle them. It implies that their existence is in a sense validated through their union with Rome, whereas they have all long traditions as independent Churches.

16 *The Messenger*, January 1980.

Western Church could assist the Pope in his ministry to the universal Church. One of the titles of the Pope, Coventry was quoted as saying, 'is Patriarch of the West. If leadership could be devolved to new patriarchs in areas of the West, diversity in the Catholic Church would be promoted and it would be easier to see the papacy as a centre for the communion of Churches.' The Pope, he added, had recently said that reunion with the Orthodox would not mean uniformity, implying that the same could be true of reunion with the Anglican Communion.[17]

Further encouragement from a Jesuit ecumenist to members of the Catholic League came in a lecture by Fr Edward (Ted) Yarnold SJ, entitled 'Ministry and Ordination: A Mutual Recognition', delivered at a conference sponsored by the League in conjunction with the Friars of the Atonement, and published in *The Messenger* for May 1984. 'Mutual recognition of ministry' had of course been for the League the central problem in the creation of the Church of South India[18] and again in proposals for reunion between the Church of England and the Methodist Church.[19] As Yarnold pointed out, for Roman Catholics the major obstacle was Leo XIII's bull declaring Anglican orders to have no validity. But several of the assumptions of *Apostolicae Curae*, he suggested, were questionable. Of the doubtful issues he raised, perhaps the strongest theological argument was point 1(d):

The Bull of 1896 assumed that the deliberate introduction of a rite embodying a Protestant understanding negated the intention of ordaining bishops and priests according to the mind of Christ and the Church. However, the wrong *understanding* of a sacrament has never been held to invalidate the administration of the sacrament. The ordinal used in 1559 clearly states the *intention* of ordaining bishops, priests and deacons, in continuance of the orders established in the time of the Apostles.

---

17 *The Messenger*, September 1984.
18 See above, p. 55.
19 See above, p. 80.

Though Yarnold does not say so, this echoes St Augustine's argument against the Donatists in the early fifth century. That a correct understanding is not required is, therefore, a conviction of long standing, and not an ad hoc theologoumenon.

Yarnold's second point was what is colloquially called 'the Dutch touch', namely that a number of Anglican bishops have had, as their co-consecrators, bishops from the Old Catholic Church of Utrecht. The Old Catholic orders are recognized as valid by the Roman Catholic Church, and therefore the orders they help to confer must also be valid.

His third point was the most original. We are looking at this problem from the wrong end, he said. Instead of talking of the recognition of ministries, we should be speaking of the recognition of Churches. Vatican II's Decree on Ecumenism already insisted that the Anglican Communion has a special place because 'Catholic traditions and institutions in part continue to exist', and episcopal ministry was, he added 'the most obvious of these institutions'.[20]

Yarnold's lecture and others that have been mentioned are evidence of a more active involvement by the Catholic League in the Ecumenical Movement. This engagement was inspired at least in part by the work of ARCIC, as has been seen much reported in the pages of *The Messenger*, and in particular by its Final Report in 1981. The Final Report was presented to the two partners in the discussions, the Roman Catholic Church and the Anglican Communion, to see whether the statements within the report on authority, the Eucharist and ministry were properly in line with the two Churches' own understanding.

The Lambeth Conference was not in a position to react until its meeting in July 1988, having had to solicit the views of all the different Anglican provinces. The whole response –

---

20 In the light of *Dominus Iesus*, the document produced by the Congregation for the Doctrine of the Faith (CDF) when the then Cardinal Josef Ratzinger, the future Benedict XVI, was its Prefect, Yarnold's claim was a bold one. The CDF's statement denied the title of 'Church' to all 'ecclesial communities' apart from those in the Orthodox tradition, and to the Old Catholics. The implications of the 'Dutch touch' were not discussed. This document was of course not known to Yarnold.

Resolution 8 of the Conference – is too long to reproduce here, but, with some caveats in particular over language, the Conference agreed that the Final Report represented the faith of the Church. Not so the CDF, in its response on behalf of the Roman Catholic Church at the end of 1991.[21] It found that the Final Report 'does not yet constitute a substantial and explicit agreement on some essential elements of Catholic faith':

a) because the Report explicitly recognizes that one or another Catholic dogma is not accepted by our Anglican brethren (for example, Eucharistic adoration, infallibility, the Marian dogmas);

b) because one or another Catholic doctrine is only accepted in part by our Anglican brethren (for example, the primacy of the Bishop of Rome);

c) because certain formulations in the Report are not explicit enough to ensure that they exclude interpretations not in harmony with the Catholic faith (for example, that which concerns the Eucharist as sacrifice, the Real Presence, the nature of the priesthood);

d) because certain affirmations in the Report are inexact and not acceptable as Catholic doctrine (for example, the relationship between the primacy and the structure of the Church, the doctrine of 'reception');

e) finally because some important aspects of the teaching of the Catholic Church have either not been dealt with or have been only in an indirect way (for example, apostolic succession, the 'regula fidei', moral teaching).

To many, this appeared a disappointingly negative response, though many of the Catholic League would have sympathized with a number of the points made in the CDF document, which

21 http://www.vatican.va/roman_curia/pontifical_councils/chrstuni/angl-comm-docs/rc_pc_chrstuni_doc_1991_catholic-response-arcici_en.html [accessed 28 October 2016]. The tardiness of the Roman Catholic response, contrasted with that of the Anglican Communion, was criticized by Brooke Lunn in 'ARCIC I – A Shock Reaction' (*The Messenger*, February 1992): 'Excuses have been made for the RC response. How can we excuse the inexcusable?"

did, nonetheless, encourage further sessions of the Commission to discuss what it saw as unresolved issues.

Long before the CDF's document was published, Fr Peter Sanderson, Director of the League's Apostleship of Prayer, had commented that 'On the one hand there has been phenomenal progress over the past ten years, especially at the theological level. On the other hand, there is a certain inertia, if not pessimism, about the contemporary state of play. Ground which has been gained looks like being lost again, due not least to the perennial Anglican weakness of equivocation.' These remarks appeared in the January 1982 issue of *The Messenger*, just before the visit of Pope (now St) John Paul II to Britain, a visit which almost did not happen because of the outbreak of the Falklands War between Britain and Argentina. Fr Sanderson's concern was what sort of image of Anglicanism would be presented to the Pontiff:

> How shall we be represented to him? Will the external image of an Established Church, a product of the Reformation, with a 'distinct and separate' identity, appearance and administration be all that manifests itself? Or will he see beyond this, a Church within a Church, the true Soul, Catholic and Roman by inheritance, albeit loyal to the Queen and Canterbury, yet tied and committed by history and Formularies to the Church which Christ founded on St Peter? Will the cry, echoing down four centuries of separation, sounding clear in the Catholic Revival, become articulate in the words of Thorndyke, 'I insist on such a principle as may serve to reunite us to Rome!' Corporate Reunion – United, not absorbed – can this be fulfilled?

The Messenger for May 1982 prepared its readers for the visit by printing the papal itinerary and publishing an article by Professor Henry Chadwick on 'The Church of England and the Pope'. Christopher Colvin, the administrator of the Anglican shrine at Walsingham, reflected that many Anglicans still nursed grievances against Rome, grievances which, he thought, had lost all meaning since Vatican II. It is often painful, he said, to discover how anti-Roman and uninformed so many Anglicans were, and as far as priests were concerned, how nervous they were about the validity of their orders. Cardinal Basil Hume was quoted from an address to the Free Church Federal Council saying that the Pope was coming 'as a pastor and a bishop and also as a pilgrim for Christian unity, and poses no threat to national or religious independence' – the last an odd thing to remark, because it is difficult to believe that many people thought that he did. Another note drew attention to the upgrading to ambassadorial (i.e. papal nuncio) status of Monsignor Bruno Heim, hitherto the Apostolic Delegate. The UK's representation in Rome was similarly enhanced.

The visit of the Pope to Britain from 28 May to 2 June 1982 proved to be highly successful, not least because, for the most part, the sun shone. It had a strongly ecumenical slant, with visits by the Pope to Canterbury Cathedral where he prayed with Archbishop Robert Runcie, and to Liverpool's Anglican Cathedral where he attended a service. In addition, he met leaders of the main Churches in the United Kingdom, and also the Chief Rabbi. The Catholic League was represented at the service in Canterbury by Fr Raymond Avent, the Priest Director, who was given a prominent seat at the front of the nave.

7

Congregation of the English Mission

While the papal visit undoubtedly gave an impetus to ecumenical discussions, as related earlier, the major hindrance to relations with the Church of England as far as Rome was concerned remained the possibility of the ordination of women, already a reality in some provinces of the Anglican Communion. In 1985 that possibility came a step closer with permission being given for the promotion of women to the diaconate – the first women deacons were ordained two years later. It had been expected that there would be a flood of people leaving the C of E for the Church of Rome, but as Michael Woodgate remarked, it was a trickle rather than a flood. And it was not simply a matter of the ordination of women, he added. When Anglo-Catholics see Hans Küng and liberation theologians being summoned to Rome to answer for their views, people 'feel encouraged to go [over to Rome] where the voice is'. There was always the chance – 'highly unlikely if not impossible' – that the Roman Catholic Church would follow the same path, there were RCs calling for it, but it would be done with the authority of the Petrine office.[1]

Otherwise life within the League went on for a while much as before. Members were reminded that they had to accept the faith of the Catholic Church as defined by the Church's Councils, up to and including Vatican II. They were, as before, encouraged to make retreats or to go on pilgrimages – in 1987 the shrine to the Blessed Virgin Mary at Fatima in Portugal was

---

1 *The Messenger*, May 1985. In 2016 Pope Francis set up a commission to study the possibility of ordaining women deacons in the Roman Catholic Church.

added to the list.[2] Fynes Clinton's desire for corporate reunion with Rome which, with women's ordination very much on the Church of England's agenda, perhaps seemed to some further away than ever, became very much a League priority. Following Fynes's penchant for creating committees within committees, at the suggestion of Brooke Lunn in March 1987 the committee of the League set up a Committee for Corporate Reunion with a brief

to promote, encourage and facilitate corporate action by all Anglicans who

1) Give priority to the cause of Christian unity
2) Are placed under increasing pressure by the continuing failure of the Church of England to maintain an unequivocal stand in the fundamental areas of Christian faith and morals
3) Are unable to accept the Church of England divisive action in rejecting the historic ministry through the 'ordination' [sic] of women
4) Wish to continue to witness faithfully to 'the legitimate prestige and the worthy patrimony of piety and usage proper to the Anglican Church' (Pope Paul VI at the Canonisation of the Forty Martyrs on 25 October 1970)
5) Wish to avoid at all costs the development of a separatist group, and so wish actively to pursue corporate reunion with Rome.

The first act of this new committee was to set up a '"counselling service" for those who increasingly feel the need to do something, but are unsure as to what they should do'. The 'contact' for this counselling service was to be Fr Michael Woodgate, now rector of Fynes Clinton's old church, St Magnus the Martyr.[3] What might be this 'patrimony' mentioned by Pope

---

2 The Ecumenical Friends of Fatima Association is still going, but independent of the League.

3 *The Messenger*, May 1987. Fr Michael Woodgate was regarded as one of the foremost Anglo-Catholic spiritual directors and confessors and Superior of the Society of Retreat Conductors. He later became a Roman

Paul had been a topic of some discussion, the summary out-
come of which was reported in *The Messenger* for May 1986.
It 'has always been expressed in loyalty to what was believed to
be in accordance with sound learning and tradition'.

The year 1988 was the seventy-fifth anniversary of the foundation of the Catholic League. It was a time for reflection on the
League's past – in the September 1983 issue of *The Messenger*
Brooke Lunn reprinted an extract from what Fynes Clinton had
written in 1933 to mark the centenary of the Oxford Movement
about corporate reunion – and on its aims and achievements.
The programme of events for the anniversary year included
the customary annual retreat, a pilgrimage to Walsingham,
what was described as a 'Catholic Event for the Lambeth
Conference' and a solemn Mass at St Magnus the Martyr to
be presided over by the Bishop of Plymouth, the Right Revd
Kenneth Newing: the Mass was to be on 1 October 1988.
Before it occurred, however, Bishop Newing had resigned his
see to become a Benedictine monk at Elmore Abbey. Instead
of the advertised sermon by Bishop Newing, the gathering
was addressed in the afternoon by the Revd Christopher Hill,
then the Archbishop of Canterbury's Secretary for Ecumenical Affairs and later Bishop of Guildford. An interview with
him was published in the June 1988 *The Messenger*, billed as
the 'Seventy-Fifth Anniversary Issue', which also contained a
message from the Archbishop of Canterbury, Robert Runcie.
'In the past', he noted, 'the ecumenism for which the Catholic
League has stood has often been regarded as beyond the fringe.
Yet the League saw that the search for unity without a search
for full communion with the See of Rome, is one sided. Since the
Second Vatican Council and the work of the Anglican–Roman
Catholic International commission many more Anglicans now
recognise this, but it is good to be able to pay tribute to the
League for this important insight.'

Catholic priest and served for a time as spiritual director at the Wonersh
seminary.

In his interview – conducted by Brooke Lunn – Christopher Hill had made the same point, though expressed rather more graphically:

> There have been Anglicans, a small number which has included the Catholic League, who have seen that unity must entail some form of universal primacy and that unity cannot be achieved without the involvement of the Roman Catholic Church. That of course, was not felt by any but a tiny minority of Anglicans until relatively recently. To think about unity involving some form of universal ministry exercised by the Bishop of Rome was regarded as a viewpoint characteristic of the 'looney right' of the Church of England!

It was to sentiments such as these, especially as voiced by the Archbishop of Canterbury, that the Priest Director referred during his Anniversary Sermon, preached on 2 July 1988 at the parish church in Corringham, Essex, 75 years to the day after the first meeting at the Holborn Restaurant. 'What the League stood for was greatly misunderstood in those days', he claimed. 'Today we may smile as we remember some of the expressions of Catholic Faith which we and our fellow Roman Catholics used and even believed essential in days past – and even sympathize with our fellow Anglicans who could not cope with the package we were offering them', Fr Avent went on to say, though it could be debated whether the League's position was indeed misunderstood or at the time simply not found acceptable by other members of the Church of England.

One Anglican who certainly did not find it acceptable was Richard Holloway, at the time Bishop of Edinburgh, shortly to become Primus of the Scottish Episcopal Church. He launched a stinging attack on Anglo-Papalism in a review of the sociologist W. S. F. Pickering's *Anglo-Catholicism*,[4] one of the few books on Anglicanism to make specific mention, if only briefly, of the Catholic League. Holloway has critical remarks to make on the book itself, particularly about Pickering's approach to

---

4 *Anglo-Catholicism: A Study in Ambiguity* (London: Routledge, 1989). The review appeared in the *Church Times* for 23 June 1989.

his topic, which Holloway appears to think is not scholarly enough. But his sharpest barbs are aimed at Anglo-Papalism:

> The ambiguities or contradictions abound in [Anglo-Catholicism], but Dr Pickering concentrates on three of them. The central ambiguity lies in claiming an exclusively Catholic identity for the Church of England and pretending that its Protestant identity does not exist or is a temporary aberration. This contradiction is seen most dramatically among the Anglo-Papalists, who live in a sort of Alice-in-Wonderland Church in which reality is what they make it. The paradoxical effect of this confusion is to make Anglo-Catholicism essentially a sect in sociological terms, though its whole self-understanding is built on its Catholic ecclesiology.
>
> A related contradiction is Anglo-Catholicism's proverbial elevation of the apostolic ministry to an almost idolatrous eminence while having a hearty contempt for most of the actual holders of the apostolic office in the Church of England. Anglo-Catholics have been great upholders of proper authority in theory, while they have played around with private preferences with all the passion of extreme Protestants.

The third 'ambiguity' of which Holloway accused Anglo-Catholicism, based on Pickering's observations, was the question of clerical celibacy, with which he associated accusations of homosexuality, and what he described as 'endless opportunities for dressing up'. He ends the review, 'There are many of us who owe our faith to Anglo-Catholicism. From it we have caught something of the beauty and compassion of God, and we are saddened by its current decline into negativism and structural contradiction.' This is a little disingenuous. In an interview he gave to *The Scotsman* newspaper in February 2012 to mark the publication of his autobiography, *Leaving Alexandria*, he claimed to have lost his faith long before he came to write this review.[5] This fact – if it is a fact –

---

5 http://www.scotsman.com/lifestyle/culture/books/interview-richard-holloway-writer-broadcaster-and-former-bishop-of-edinburgh-in-the-scottish-episcopal-church-1-2140139 [accessed 18 September 2016].

was obviously unknown to Brooke Lunn who responded to the *Church Times*'s piece in an article in *The Messenger* of October 1989. He finds in (the then Bishop) Holloway 'in his heart or in his subconscious a reaching out towards the fullness of the Church as proclaimed in mainstream Christianity'.

Lunn rejected Holloway's criticisms in turn. He had no difficulty in demonstrating that 'the official formularies' of the Church of England assert its Catholic identity, and he quoted a 'scholar in our tradition, the historian Dr T. M. Parker', who had written that both the C of E and English Roman Catholicism 'are descendants of the pre-reformation Church. To treat either as the sole descendant is unsupportable.' On the third contradiction – which Lunn agrees is a stereotype – he says there is no research to support the accusation, but points out that Anglo-Papalists must uphold the traditional moral teaching of the Church.

These comments appeared in the last issue of *The Messenger* to be published while Fr Raymond Avent was the Priest Director of the Catholic League. In the same issue, Fr Philip Gray, vicar of Mendlesham in Suffolk, in his capacity as the Director of the League's Apostleship of Prayer, added to the Apostleship's list of prayers an intercession for the Council of the League, which on 11 October was to select Fr Avent's successor.

The successor was Philip Gray himself, a member of the League since 1962 and Director of the Apostleship of Prayer since 1983. In his first editorial, he thanked his predecessor for his service to the League and in particular for his work on the revision of the Constitution, bringing it into line with the decrees of Vatican II. He also asked the League to pray for the committee, and in the Apostleship of Prayer section he named them. Some members, he said, not making it clear whether he was talking of the League at large or just the committee, feel isolated, and so provided an indication of the whereabouts of committee members – though short of full addresses – so that they could be personally contacted. Of those listed, 18, including the Director, were clergy, while 8 were lay people, divided equally male and female. The committee members were reasonably well scattered throughout the country, but there was a clear predominance from the London area.

The prayer list also mentioned the constituent societies of the League: the Sodality of the Precious Blood (for celibate clergy), the Apostleship of Prayer, the Congregation of the English Mission – of which more below – and Fynes Clinton's Fraternity of Our Lady de Salve.[6] The League was itself part of a number of organizations: the Friends of the Anglican Centre in Rome, the Church Union and the Society of Our Lady of Egmanton.

This last requires a little explaining. There had been a medieval devotion to Our Lady of Egmanton, a small village in Nottinghamshire, not far from Newark, but not on the scale of Walsingham. When the church in the village was renovated by Ninian Comper between 1895 and 1897, a statue of the Virgin and Child was erected, one of the first in the country in an Anglican parish church, and a Guild of Our Lady of Egmanton instituted to maintain the shrine, to be succeeded by the Society of Our Lady of Egmanton. From 1929 there had been regular pilgrimages to the shrine, though the first formal one arranged by the Catholic League did not take place until October 1991. From then on it became an annual event.[7]

In the penultimate paragraph of his editorial, Fr Gray commented on the ordination of women, still at that point some way off. He remarked that some might be tempted to leave the Church of England and become Roman Catholics. He advised against it, quoting a letter he had received in March 1962 when he had himself been considering the Roman option. The letter was from Fr Clive Beresford, the Priest Director who had received him into the Catholic League:

Of course you will get bouts of Roman Fever – we all do, and certainly I have had my share in the past. I am pretty sure that it has to be resisted – for one thing I am perfectly certain about is that God has placed us where we are for a very

6 See above, p. 22.

7 Yelton, *Anglican Papalism*, pp. 144–7. Though the League's pilgrimage took place in October, the main pilgrimage to Egmanton was, and remains, that for the feast of the Assumption, 15 August.

definite reason; we have to be the 'leaven' which pervades the whole rather curious lump we call the C. of E. Every time one of us 'goes over', he MAY be satisfying himself, but he can no longer work in the same way, and those of us who are left have all the tougher job because we have lost some of the 'leaven' ... I am sure we must not be surprised on resentful when these things happen in the C. of E. – it is all part of the symptoms of the real disease which is, of course, our separation from Peter. And if anything in this world is worth doing, it must surely be the efforts that convinced Catholics make for the healing of that dreadful schism.

These thoughts, Gray believed, were as applicable in 1990 as they had been when they were first written.[8]

Meanwhile the Catholic League had appointed its first Information Officer. A committee member had suggested that the 'Catholic Movement' had failed to build on Archbishop Robert Runcie's 1989 visit to Pope John Paul II, a task which might have been done by someone with the remit to liaise with the press. When he came to be given his remit, however, it was rather wider: his task was to address the hostility of Roman Catholics to the Church of England, to advise on lobbies on national issues – the lobby against the Embryology Bill was specifically mentioned – which the League might wish to attend, to foster joint RC/C of E events and to monitor the use of the word 'Catholic' by non-RC groups.[9]

---

8 Philip Gray published a short account of the shrine in *The Messenger* for June 1991.

9 Another innovation around this time was the appointment of a President, an office allowed for in the Constitution but which had never been filled. When in 1996 Fr Kevin Eastell, who had promoted the League in the North of England in a valiant effort to make it seem less London-based, resigned from the committee to take up a post in France, Geoffrey Wright, the General Secretary, suggested that, rather than disappear entirely, he might become President with the remit to advise the Council and Priest Director on constitutional matters in the event of any appeal or disagreement. When Eastell had to resign the office through ill health he was succeeded, in 2009, by Fr Michael Rear, who has described the post as a largely honorific position although – he added – the League cannot be disbanded without the President's approval.

As the vote to allow the ordination of women within the Church of England came closer, *The Messenger* seemed to take on a more expressly Roman Catholic feel, with regular appearances in its pages of articles by RC clergy, especially Jesuits. In October 1991, for instance, the magazine marked both the start of Pope John Paul's Decade of Evangelism and of the Ignatian Year, marking the 450th anniversary of the formal establishment of the Society of Jesus. And above all there was an increasingly urgent pressure to establish closer bonds with Roman Catholicism, and with English Roman Catholicism in particular.

The Committee for Corporate Reunion mentioned above[10] held an informal meeting with Fr Michael Seed, a Franciscan Friar of the Atonement – the Graymoor Friars, founded by Fr Paul Wattson[11] – who was the Ecumenical Officer of the Archbishop of Westminster, Cardinal Basil Hume. The meeting took place in November 1987, some ten months after the Committee had been established. In September 1988, however, the Council of the League recommended that the Committee for Corporate Reunion be dissolved to be replaced by a more formal structure, known as the Congregation of the English Mission (CEM). Provisional statutes for the CEM were drawn up and a commentary on them provided. The first of the statutes describes the CEM as 'a secular society, clerical and lay, whose purpose is the greater glory of God, particularly through the proclamation of the Gospel to the English people'. There were more meetings, always denominated as informal, with the Vatican's Congregation for the Doctrine of the Faith, again with Westminster's Ecumenical Officer and with the Apostolic Pro-Nuncio, Archbishop Luigi Barbarito.[12]

---

10 See p. 95.

11 See above p. 44.

12 In diplomatic protocol, a papal nuncio is automatically dean of the diplomatic corps in each country. Where this was not thought appropriate, normally in predominantly non-Roman Catholic countries, he was called pro-nuncio. In 1993 Archbishop Barbarito became the longest-serving diplomat accredited to the Court of St James, thereby becoming dean by seniority. Subsequent papal representatives in London have all been titled nuncios.

In January 1989 the CEM held a study day, and the following month had their first meeting with the Archbishop of Westminster, Cardinal Hume, as a result of which the cardinal proposed Fr Anthony Nye, a Jesuit priest on the staff of Farm Street Church, London, along with Fr Seed as discussion partners: CEM's side was represented by Brooke Lunn, who had been the first to propose setting up the CEM, Fr Michael Woodgate and the League's Secretary, Mr Geoffrey Wright. There were two more study days and a further meeting with the cardinal.

The CEM's report, published in *The Messenger* for October 1990, is illuminating, and as far as ecumenical relations are concerned, never more so than in the paragraph headed 'An English RC View of Anglicans', which is worth quoting in full:

Perhaps the most significant and difficult lesson we have learnt in these last three years is the overwhelmingly negative view that many RCs have of Anglicanism. Our RC friends have been clear on this. In the light of this, our reading of Vatican 2, the statements of the Popes, and RC ecumenical statements in general appear [*sic*] to have been naïve. The gap between official statements and what English RCs actually feel is substantial. We forbear to detail this negative view here, but clearly there is a great need to develop mutual knowledge, understanding and trust where these are largely absent. This negative attitude is a major factor in the inability of RCs to begin to understand or cope with the mainstream Papalist position.

By saying that they 'forbear to detail this negative view here', the report's authors skirt the question as to why RCs have such attitudes. It might have been helpful for future relations to have done so, as one of the convictions of the Catholic League, that the Church of England was in a direct line of descent from the Church which St Augustine brought to Canterbury in 597 – which the report avoids stating directly though it hints at it – would be toxic to most 'cradle' Roman Catholics. They had very likely been taught from childhood that the C of E was radically discontinuous from the Church represented by St

Augustine, and that it was *created* by Henry VIII's decision to break with the papacy in pursuit of a divorce from Katherine of Aragon.[13]

The report nevertheless could point to some considerable improvement in relations between the two Churches. RCs were, in living memory, forbidden even to join in the Lord's Prayer with Anglicans,[14] but now there were 'shared churches, shared schools and many other examples of cooperation'. In this context, the notion of a Uniate status for Anglicans within Roman Catholicism was rejected – as Andrew Louth had pointed out,[15] the cultural differences that marked off such communities did not apply to the situation in Britain.[16] They had next proposed that they should be incorporated as a 'personal prelature', a structure envisaged in the Vatican II Decree on the Ministry and Life of Priests, and brought into being by Pope Paul VI's Apostolic Letter *Ecclesiae Sanctae* of August 1966. A personal prelature can perhaps be best described as a diocese which had no geographical limits, and as such had been used only once, to provide a juridical status for the RC organization known as Opus Dei, which looked like, but strictly speaking was not, a religious order. 'We were swiftly told that personal prelatures were anathema, and that a different model was necessary', remarks the report.[17] 'We need to be integrated with the English

13 One might also add that many of the contemporary RC community had some kind of link with Ireland, where the Anglican Church of Ireland was associated with the oppression of the Ascendancy.

14 Or indeed with any non-RCs. On praying the Lord's Prayer with other Christians, a practice known as *communicatio in sacris* and as such once forbidden by Rome, see my two-part article, 'Ecumenism in War-Time Britain', *Heythrop Journal* 23 (1982), pp. 234–58, 377–94.

15 See above p. 87.

16 In an address to the CEM published in *The Messenger*, June 1991, the same point was made by Fr Roman Cholij, Vice-Chancellor of the Ukrainian Apostolic Exarchate in Britain: 'I hope to have demonstrated', he said in conclusion, 'that the Uniate model cannot be an appropriate one for Anglican union, if only for the reason that the historical and ecclesial heritage of the Anglican church and today's Roman Catholic Church in England are not sufficiently dissimilar.'

17 For Opus Dei, see my *The Secret World of Opus Dei* (London: Grafton Books, 1989). There is a discussion of personal prelatures in relation to Opus on pp. 80–3. Personal prelatures – at least the one that was created

RCs in one hierarchy', concluded the report's authors. Finally, they had a word to say on the term 'convert':

> We have stated our belief that [the word] only properly applies to conversion from sin and evil to Jesus Christ our Lord and saviour. To suggest that we wish to convert from Anglicanism to Roman Catholicism is totally unacceptable to us. These are not two mutually exclusive faiths. We believe that the great benefits we have received as Anglicans are not to be renounced or rejected. We do not feel we have yet succeeded in conveying this conviction to our RC friends.

And as if to illustrate the point, *The Messenger's* editor, Fr Brooke Lunn, printed a sermon reached by the cardinal at the ordination as a Roman Catholic priest of the former Anglican priest, Philip Goff,[18] on 10 July 1990, followed by a suggestion as to what Basil Hume might have said, had he shown appropriate sensitivity to the League's understanding of their position. Fr Nye, the League's Cardinal Hume appointed interlocutor, saw things rather differently. He had himself been an Anglican and had become a Roman Catholic in the early 1950s. He took part in several discussions with League members and attended a couple of meetings. Looking back on the experience nearly 30 years later, he confessed he had not been impressed. 'They were looking for ways to stay where they were', he said, and did not mind being quoted.[19]

On 11 November 1992, by a two-thirds majority of each of the three Houses of the General Synod, the Church of England voted to approve that which the Catholic League most feared: the admission of women to the priesthood. The decision taken, it was greeted with rejoicing both in the gallery of the chamber and in Dean's Yard outside Church House 'where a huge

---

– proved to be unpopular with the local hierarchy because the bishops had very little control over its activities. It was particularly unpopular with Cardinal Hume – again, see my book, pp. 164–5.

18 Fr Goff subsequently returned to the ministry of the Church of England.

19 Private conversation, 14 December 2016.

cheer was raised. At the same time, for very many of us who were listening to the radio or watching the live television coverage, the dismay and disbelief reduced us to utter silence.'[20] In a letter to members, dated 25 November, Geoffrey Wright, the League's Secretary General, referred to the decision as being taken on 'Black Wednesday', and on 28 November, the League's Priest Director, Philip Gray, together with Geoffrey Wright, issued a statement on behalf of the League:

> The Catholic League deeply regrets the decision. We believe that the Church of England, as a result of the vote on November 11th, lacks
> 1. Unity in Faith by the rejection of the Catholic Tradition,
> 2. Unity in Sacraments in proposing to legislate to change the nature, effects and conditions of validity, and
> 3. Unity in Authority because when a bishop ordains a woman the unity of the Church in that diocese will be destroyed.

This appeared in the February 1993 issue of *The Messenger*, together with a number of other expressions of dismay, including one from the editor, Brooke Lunn, which could scarcely have been more forthright, addressed to his parishioners at Holy Trinity, Stroud Green: 'We can't change God's truth by a majority vote, the most we can change is where we stand in relation to God's truth. The vote of the General Synod of the Church of England on 11th November 1992 was a vote of no confidence in our Lord and Master Jesus Christ.'

There were, as has been said, a number of contributions, but Brooke Lunn appears to have written the greater part of the issue, including that advertised as the response of the Congregation for the English Mission. There had to be, he wrote, a reconciliation of the differing 'faith stories' of the Church of England and English Roman Catholicism: 'we need', he said, 'to acknowledge that they, like us, are legitimate descendants of the pre-sixteenth-century Church in England. In this way

---

20 David Houlding, 'The Crisis of 1992 and Its Aftermath: A Personal Reflection', in *In This Sign Conquer*, pp. 196–217.

we need to rid ourselves of any false preconceptions we might have.' A critic might comment that one of those false preconceptions was that English RCs would readily recognize the C of E as a legitimate descendant of pre-sixteenth-century English Catholicism. When he wrote that English RCs view Anglicans 'with a mixture of suspicion and resentment', he put this down to three factors: (1) that Anglicans are doctrinally and morally woolly, (2) that they tend to question authority and (3) 'they resent what they perceive as an assumed superiority ... deriving largely from the Establishment and all that flows from it'. While Anglicans might find becoming RCs an apparently attractive proposition, they would not find so attractive 'entry into the English RC culture', he argued – displaying, one might have thought, exactly that sense of Anglican superiority he had just suggested the English RCs would resent.

The next issue of *The Messenger*, that of June 1993, proved controversial – in the October committee meeting it was decided that a note should appear in the forthcoming *Messenger* making it clear that the views expressed did not reflect the opinions of the members of the committee. The editor, Brooke Lunn, had himself made the point in an editorial headed 'No Apologies': 'the views expressed in this issue are personal and not the agreed expression of the members of the League. However, in talking with officers and other members, these views seem to be widely shared even if the particular expression of them is very personal. For this I make no apologies.' And he added, 'The situation remains new, but the various responses to it have nothing new about them.'

The officers of the League had written to the Roman Catholic Bishops of England and Wales in advance of their annual meeting in Low Week. There was no direct response from the RC hierarchy, but on St George's Day they issued a lengthy statement. This made it quite clear that there was to be no move towards corporate reunion. All that was on offer was individual reception into the local RC community through the customary process, even in situations where whole groups wished to join the Roman Catholic Church. A letter from the Archbishops of Canterbury and York welcomed 'this pastorally sensitive statement', but that was definitely not how it was seen by Lunn: rather it was a 'Miscalculation', arising, he suggested, from the mistaken belief that Catholic Anglicans had come to the end of the road. On this interpretation, they had no alternative but to become RCs. Not true, said Lunn, they could stay exactly where they were. 'Sacramental full communion between the two episcopal hierarchies may be further away than ever, but otherwise we seem to have here a full communion of sweetness and light. Meanwhile, the people languish.' The behaviour of the English RC hierarchy, he went on, is 'in the traditional understanding of the term in the Church, a scandal', and he had an explanation. Anglicans in England, he said, are centre stage whereas the RC bishops were in the wings, something they resented.

The committee meeting in October 1993 recorded that they had received expressions of concern about the tenor of the June issue, and asked for a note to be inserted which distanced the committee itself from views expressed by Lunn – though, as has been remarked, he had insisted that the opinions were his own.[21] A note to that effect finally appeared, but the request came too late for the October issue, the content of which continued the debate, though in a more moderate tone. The first article advanced the argument for a 'Third Province' within England with episcopal oversight by a bishop in the Catholic tradition. It was advanced by a member of the Forward in Faith movement, which eventually achieved this aim. In its beginnings, Forward in Faith asked for, and received, a donation from the League of £5,000, a substantial slice of its cash holdings at the time.[22] The League, however, later expressed reservations about Forward in Faith, which while certainly in the Catholic tradition had proved not to be satisfactorily papalist.

---

21 The February 1994 issue of *The Messenger*, which contained the committee's disclaimer, was a very slim publication, and without the by now customary colour on its front cover. The disclaimer was signed by all the committee members apart from Brooke Lunn, who was not listed as editor.

22 Committee Minutes for the meeting of 10 October 1992. At the time, the League had just over £7,000 in cash.

Fr Lunn surveyed the articles and letters which had appeared in *The Tablet* as a consequence of the St George's Day statement. He took particular exception to the suggestion, supported by Ms Vicky Cosstick and Fr Oliver McTernan, that the appropriate way for the reception of Anglicans was the Rite of Christian Initiation of Adults (RCIA). This programme, Lunn judged, was suitable only for those who knew little or nothing of the Catholic faith. 'It is an incredible impertinence', he wrote in the June 1993 issue of *The Messenger*, 'to be told that we must be properly instructed.' Ms Cosstick's letter was rather more nuanced than perhaps Fr Lunn indicated. She said in part: 'The RCIA process is not an instruction by those who know of those who do not know, but a communal search, among those who share a desire to know Christ better, for the answer to the question of what it means to be a Catholic Christian in this place and time. I would be most concerned if Anglicans, whether lay or ordained, motivated to become Catholics by the November decision of the Church of England's General Synod, felt that they were somehow above or beyond, or in any way slighted by, this process. Properly understood, it is a gift to both the Church and the new members.'[23] Lunn found rather more encouragement in the article by the Jesuit Edward Yarnold and in *The Tablet*'s leader for 1 May 1993. The third paragraph of the editorial which had gained his approval read: 'The real issue, Cardinal Hume once more insisted, was not the ordination of women, but the authority of the General Synod of the Church of England to make the decision to ordain them. Yet the nature of the authority crisis among the Anglo Catholic clergy is that they believe they are Catholic priests and that the women will not be. If they were not utterly convinced that they were already Catholic priests they would not have a problem. A solution that expects them to concede on that point is for them no solution at all.'[24]

---

23 *The Tablet*, 29 May 1993, p. 688. It is perhaps worth remarking that neither the editor of *The Tablet* nor Ms Cosstick were 'cradle' Roman Catholics.

24 Ibid., 1 May 1993, p. 535. Lunn did not, however, cite the first sentence of the paragraph quoted.

But what was the solution? Anglican Papalists had long had little confidence in the Roman Catholic bishops in Britain who at every turn seemed staunchly to reject any form of corporate reunion. As has already been mentioned, both the Uniate option and that of the personal prelature had been abandoned. The only solution appeared to be incorporation into the Roman Catholic Church but with some form of independent arbiter. The suggestion was that this arbiter should be a bishop from the European Continent: in the experience of the League's members, Continental clergy were usually more welcoming than British ones perhaps because they were not as concerned as were the British with the League's claim that they were in direct descent from the pre-Reformation Catholic Church. There was also a belief, at least among some members of the League, that because, in many cases, the Roman Catholic Churches in Europe had been, or sometimes still were, national Churches, there was more understanding among them of the position of the Church of England as part of the Establishment.

8

'It is Accomplished'

After the decision by the General Synod, a number of members of the Catholic League had become Roman Catholics, joined one of the Orthodox Churches or attached themselves to what had come to be called 'continuing' Anglican Churches. On 9 October 1996, the Council issued a statement acknowledging this fact, at the same time urging those who had been members not to resign but to remain part of the League. The League, it said, would stay as it was because the Council believed only a minority of its membership would depart from the Church of England, nevertheless in future it would have an ecumenical constituency to a greater degree than in the past. Its aims and objectives had not changed, said the statement – promotion of fellowship among Catholics, the union of all Christians with the See of Rome, the spread of the Catholic faith and the deepening of the spiritual life of those who belonged to it – but one thing had certainly changed, at least according to the *Newsletter*: the phrase 'in communion with the see of Canterbury' had been deleted from the League's objectives.[1] The *Newsletter* itself was an innovation. Put together by Geoffrey Wright, the League's General Secretary, it first appeared in August 1994 and has appeared regularly three times a year in between issues of *The Messenger*, carrying news, like the earlier *Messenger*, of retreats, pilgrimages, intentions of the Apostleship of Prayer and so on. It usually also had a brief message from the Director.

---

1 *Newsletter* 7, August 1996. It was deleted after a decision taken by the Council on 4 November 1993. The League had some difficulty in persuading the Anglican council of Catholic societies that, as an ecumenical organization, it was no longer one of their number.

One Rome-ward decision the committee made on behalf of its members was to elect to the committee a married Roman Catholic priest. Another, rather odd one, was to move its by now not inconsiderable assets of some £120,000 from the funds managed by the Church of England's Central Board of Finance. They chose to place the money instead with the Westminster Diocese, after some discussion with the diocese's finance officer. It was duly moved, but it transpired that Westminster Diocese was not legally able to handle the funds, and they had to be moved back to the C of E.

Of much more significance, however, was renewed interest in the question of priestly ordination within the Church of England: were Anglican orders 'valid', despite the condemnation in Pope Leo XIII's *Apostolicae Curae*? In an article in *Reuniting Anglicans and Rome*, a special, and much enlarged, issue of *The Messenger* for October 1994, Fr John Hunwicke argued that they were. For him, the episcopal ordination of Bertram Fitzgerald Simpson in 1932 as Bishop of Kensington was the crucial starting point. One of his consecrators was the Old Catholic Bishop of Haarlem, and Simpson himself, who was translated to Southwark in 1941 and remained in post until 1959, had in the meantime taken part in very many priestly, and episcopal, ordinations. Thus, argued Hunwicke, the 'Dutch touch' passed on to very many clergy of the C of E priestly orders in the sense required for validity by Leo's bull of 1896: because Rome recognizes that the Old Catholics have valid orders, so must all those who had benefitted from the Dutch touch. When in 1994 Graham Leonard, the former Bishop of London, was ordained as a Roman Catholic priest by Cardinal Hume very soon after he had been received, also by the cardinal, into the Roman Catholic Church, the sacrament was conferred 'conditionally', just in case, as it were, his former orders had been valid and he was already a priest in the sense required by Rome.[2] The cardinal was not entirely happy about this, notes Hunwicke, and the *sub conditione* conferring of orders was not repeated.

---

2 Cf. the obituary in the *Daily Telegraph*, http://www.telegraph.co.uk/news/obituaries/6943119/The-Rt-Rev-Mgr-Graham-Leonard.html [accessed 25 November 2016].

The Westminster offer is 'absolute' ordination, but with an additional formula which makes very warm remarks about the former Anglican ministry of the individual concerned. It contains, however, the words 'your servant ... *now* seeks to be ordained to the presbyterate'; so, in effect, it constitutes an extremely polite and amazingly friendly way of affirming the certain invalidity of all Anglican Orders (Dutchmen or no Dutchmen). I do not see how, with integrity, I could take part in these proceedings.[3]

Cardinal Hume's discomfort with the *sub conditione* ceremony is understandable, given the decidedly mechanistic understanding of validity embraced by Roman Catholic sacramental theology. For someone to have valid episcopal orders, he must first have received valid presbyteral orders, which recourse to the 'Dutch touch' suggests he does not think he has. It is, in other words, something of a circular argument.[4]

Fr Hunwicke's paper in this special edition of *The Messenger* was followed by a lengthy piece by Brooke Lunn, discussing the case, as a loyal disciple of Fynes Clinton, for corporate reunion with Rome. He pointed out that there was no single corporate identity for all those seeking reunion with Rome, though the Catholic League was probably the most distinct, numerous and readily identifiable body of those that were. He acknowledged that there were several parish groups who were, or might be, in search of corporate reunion, some of them hoping to take their parish churches with them – an aspiration unlikely to be fulfilled.[5] But, as Fr Lunn pointed out, it drew attention to a fundamental difference between the Anglican and the Roman Catholic understanding of the parish, for an Anglican parish

---

3 *The Messenger*, October 1994, pp. 56–8. The quotation is on p. 58. Fr Hunwicke then provides documentation – in Latin – concerning the accord between the Old Catholic Church and the Church of England.

4 This is simply a matter of reporting: the present writer has no desire to enter this debate.

5 The *Newsletter* for August 1996 sought information on those groups who had proposed 'to take church buildings to Rome, and how they had not been successful'.

priest, unlike his RC counterpart, considered himself to be of service to all those living within his parish's boundaries, and not just to those who attended his services. He indicated further differences:

> The C. of E., with its national status, its control by the state, and the absence of incardination [the process by which RC priests come to belong to a specific diocese] tends towards seeing the local church not as the diocese but as the C. of E. The Archbishop of Canterbury therefore takes a more prominent position in relation to all the members of the C. of E. Clergy move much more freely from one diocese to another. It is therefore more meaningful to speak of Anglican identity than of English RC identity. There are other factors which might reinforce this difference. English RCs have, perforce, been largely marginalised in English society, and consequently developed a ghetto mentality. Coming out of the ghetto is a slow and problematic process. The English RC identity tends to be very much 16th century and later, as is seen in their National Calendar of Feasts. The cosmopolitan make-up of English RCs is another factor. The difference in the extent to which members of the C. of E. and English RCs perceive their corporate identity is one reason why RCs have difficulty in handling the concept of Anglican identity.[6]

One might add that, conversely, it is the reason why C of E members have difficulty in understanding RC identity, which, certainly as far as the notion of the local church is concerned, is based upon a theological principle rather than a geographical accident.

Brooke Lunn's reflections are illuminating. Together with his quotation from an off-the-cuff remark by Cardinal Hume that he – the cardinal – did not know 'how his people would cope with all these clever Anglicans',[7] an *obiter dictum* which Lunn makes much of, they help to explain what it is that, despite

---

6 *The Messenger*, October 1994, p. 72.
7 Ibid., pp. 75 and 76.

their protestations about reunion with the Holy See, kept so many Catholic members of the Church of England within the Anglican Communion.

As the need for reunion grew more pressing among Catholic Anglicans, so did the question of what precisely constituted that Anglican identity which those wishing to join the Roman Catholic Church might bring with them. The simplest answer to this might have been a 'Uniate' solution, but this, as has been seen, had already been dismissed,[8] and so, too, had the idea of a personal prelature.[9] As the Congregation of the English Mission had declared, 'We seek a common Christian identity rather than the maintenance of separate Anglican and English RC identities. We believe that there is of good value in both our separate identities which should be maintained. We believe that neither identity on its own is adequate as an English Christian identity.'[10] Lunn returned to this text in a review of *The Roman Option* by Dr William Oddie,[11] a former Anglican priest, who was on the point of taking over the editorship of *The Catholic Herald*, a post he held until 2004. He suggested that 'As part of an appropriate inculturation', the RC hierarchy should authorize, as an optional use for all, the Authorized Version, 'Specified BCP/ASB collects and other prayers', and the Coverdale translation of the Roman Canon. And, he added, there should be a revision of the National Calendar, presumably to make it more inclusive. In other words, Lunn envisaged a common identity: rather than Anglicans being absorbed wholly by the Roman Catholics, RCs would absorb something of the Anglican patrimony, a process nowadays becoming known as 'receptive ecumenism'.

---

8 Cf. above, p. 87.

9 Cf. above, p. 104. However, in an article in *The Messenger* for October 2002, Fr John Hunwicke wrote about the reunion of Lefebvrists with Rome – which did not happen – as a model that Anglicans might follow and returned again to the question of a personal prelature 'actualised in that admirable organisation Opus Dei'.

10 *The Messenger*, October 1994, p. 9.

11 *The Roman Option: The Realignment of English Christianity* (London: Harper Collins, 1997).

The June 1990 issue of *The Messenger* and the one following contained several accounts, under the heading of 'Personal
Pilgrimage', by people who had become Roman Catholics[12] – and
by some who having tested the waters returned to Anglicanism. The process of becoming an RC, said one disillusioned
would-be Roman Catholic, was 'lacking in Natural Justice and
devoid of Christian charity'. Despite printing views such as this,
the June issue was criticized for being too weighted in favour
of those who had gone over to Rome. There were clearly tensions. As Fr Philip Gray, the Priest Director, commented in the
December 1996 *Newsletter*, 'The Catholic Movement in the
Church of England has often been branded as "gin, lace and
backbiting". We all like some gin and lace, but we must not
give in to backbiting.'

The Catholic League, as its members were often reminded,
was a small organization, and getting smaller despite recruit-
ment drives. In 1995 a network of regional representatives
was revived, the representatives themselves being expected
to keep in contact with all members in their several areas of
England. But though small, in the complicated situation for
Anglo-Catholics that had arisen because of the decision by the
Church of England to ordain women, it provided information
and support, a support which was especially appreciated by
Anglicans in those parts of the country where Anglo-Catholic
parishes were few and far between. Perhaps even more important, it provided spiritual sustenance especially through the
Apostleship of Prayer and its regular pilgrimages. From 1992,
in addition to the shrines of Our Lady in England, a pilgrimage was added to Bruges, with a visit to the Basilica of the
Precious Blood being the highlight. Apart from the first couple
of years when they had rooms at the English convent, members
of the League stayed at the Begijnhof, and were permitted by
the bishop of the city to receive Communion alongside the
Sisters at Sunday Mass, and to join in their recitation of the
Divine Office: the Mother Superior established a chapel in

---

12 'The people who decided to become Roman Catholics', David Chapman has commented, 'were not those whom everyone expected' [private
conversation].

the guesthouse for eucharistic adoration and for which the League provided an icon of the Mother of God, and a suitable tabernacle and sanctuary lamp. The chapel and altar were not formally consecrated but dedicated.

A major change in the League's life occurred in 2000. From the beginning, the League had embraced a statement of the Catholic faith to which members were expected to adhere. At first this was the creed of the Council of Trent,[13] but this was changed to Pope Paul VI's 1968's *Credo of the People of God*[14] and shortly afterwards to the whole body of the Councils of the Church, including the Second Vatican Council. As Robert Farmer noted in a short article in *The Messenger* in June 2000, digesting all the Councils was rather a big challenge for the League's members. It was proposed instead that the faith to which members were committed was to be more conveniently found in the *Catechism of the Catholic Church*, first published in 1994 and just recently (1999) revised.[15]

While this might have been taken by some as a sign of increasing affinity between the Catholic League and the Church of Rome, there was a sobering sermon to be read in the December 2000 issue of *The Messenger* – read, because the Priest Director had intended to deliver it at the Annual General Meeting of the League at St Silas, Kentish Town on 7 November, but he had been prevented by floods from attending:

I have to confess that I can no longer remember what it feels like to be hopeful about the corporate reunion of the Church of England with the Catholic Church.[16] I still have my ticket giving me admission to the precinct of Canterbury Cathedral in May 1982 when the Holy Father and the Archbishop of

---

13 Cf. above, p. 24.

14 Cf. above, p. 76.

15 This change had been incorporated into the revision of the Constitution while Raymond Avent was the Priest Director. Avent was assisted in the revision by Aidan Harker, at one time a monk of Nashdom.

16 Hitherto members of the League writing in any of its publications had been careful to speak of the Roman Catholic, rather than just the Catholic, Church, as Fr Philip Gray does here. From this point onwards, however, 'Catholic Church' became more common.

Canterbury jointly enthroned the Book of the Gospels in the chair of St Augustine in the Cathedral. Though we were sworn to secrecy then, perhaps it need no longer be covered up that earlier that morning in the crypt of the Cathedral the Dean and assorted Anglican dignitaries (some bishops) concelebrated a Mass together with visiting Roman Catholic dignitaries – abbots and bishops among them – though no Englishmen I think.

A similarly depressing assessment is to be found in two articles in the October 2005 and June 2006 issues of *The Messenger* by Canon F. E. Pickard. The first contains forthright criticism of the Roman Catholic Church ('One thing that can be said with certainty is that the Roman Catholic Church is NOT the Catholic Church of the land: it is a chaplaincy for the Émigré, and primarily for the Irish'), the second article calls for a revival of the Catholic movement within the Church of England and the role of the Catholic League within it:

> To a certain extent, the lesser battle is already won. Most Catholic clergy are *de facto* Papalists, whether they are formal members [of the League] or not. Those who are not of this mind are largely departed to Affirming Catholicism already. So far as the Church of England at large is concerned, we need first to work with a remotivated Catholic body as I have suggested. We then deploy our resources to remind the church that the historic place of the English Church is as part of the Church of the West and that ultimately, nothing less will do. I myself believe that we need to say to the Catholic Movement, that the evidence is clear that individual cessions have achieved nothing: corporate reunion is the only viable objective.

With the benefit of hindsight, this seems remarkably old fashioned, but Canon Pickard had opened his piece with the words 'First, it isn't raining yet. We are unlikely to see ladies "ordained" to the Episcopate for a year or two, perhaps several', and to that extent he was correct: the ordination of a woman to the episcopate was not authorized until 2014, the first being consecrated a year later.

The first decade of the twenty-first century was a time of considerable turbulence in the League's affairs. In June 2002 Mr Geoffrey Wright, the long-serving Secretary General, who was sometimes known as 'Roman Wright', died very suddenly, throwing the administration into confusion though happily for a fairly short time. Nonetheless, some records were lost when his flat was cleared. Then, on 1 September 2003, Philip Gray stepped down as Priest Director, to be succeeded by Fr Robert Farmer who served for only a year. At the suggestion of David Chapman, who replaced Geoffrey Wright as Secretary, he was followed by Brooke Lunn, recently retired from his London parish of Stroud Green.

Lunn was, Chapman commented, a man of forthright opinions which were not easily shaken.[17] He was also a direct link with Fynes Clinton, whose Mass he had regularly served at St Magnus the Martyr. Lunn promptly instituted a number of reforms. The website was revamped and renamed, becoming http://www.unitas.co.uk, taking the title used for the *Newsletter*. There was also a restructuring of the Council which, it was generally agreed, had become too large to be efficient. It was replaced by an Executive, the members of which were to have a three-year term. The Annual General Meeting on 3 March 2008 approved the proposals and elected the first Executive – Priest Director, General Secretary, Treasurer, membership secretary, website secretary and pilgrimage secretary. The officers were empowered to co-opt a maximum of three others from the membership, which they did. The Executive Committee was now also the Trustee Committee of Unitas–Catholic League, with Brooke Lunn as its Priest Director. From October 1989 Lunn had also been the editor of *The Messenger*, but he relinquished that role in 2007 with a note in the October issue of that year headed 'VALE'. 'I take my leave', he said, 'with many memories, mostly good.' The Committee instituted a survey to determine the future of the magazine – how often

---

17 Private conversation.

did members read it, they wanted to know. It went out to the 550 members: three submitted written replies, one made a phone call.

Then, to everyone's astonishment and to the confusion of the Executive, Brooke Lunn resigned as well: his name no longer appeared as Priest Director in the December 2008 edition of the *Newsletter*. He was replaced, at first in an acting capacity, by Mark Woodruff, a long-standing member of the League but by this time a Roman Catholic priest. Perhaps the Executive should not have been surprised. In the August 2008 issue of the *Newsletter* Lunn wrote:

> Is it totally unrealistic for me to dream that all that is of good value in the Anglican faith story will not be just thrown away and discarded? Might I dream of the Church in England – Anglicans, Methodists, Catholics, Free Churchmen – united with each other and with the Roman Apostolic See, and that all that is of good value in our several heritages shared with each other?

After the Church of England's decision to ordain women to the episcopate,[18] wrote Mark Woodruff in the same issue of the *Newsletter*,

> Division between the Anglican Church and its Catholic and Orthodox ecumenical partners in preference to this search for communion has taken permanent, solid form. We have now entered a new situation in the movement towards Church unity. The old paradigm of reunion for the Catholic and Anglican Churches on the basis of Episcopal structures to be mutually 'united, not absorbed' has come to an end.
>
> Some will be looking to reconciliation on a corporate basis. It is well known that there is a wariness about this among Catholics in England, partly through a fear of a multiplication

18 Formal authority to consecrate women bishops was, of course, not conceded until 2014, the first consecration occurring the following year. What had happened in 2008 was a Synod vote to remove any final legal obstacles to the consecration of women bishops. There still remained the problem of what to do, in terms of ecclesiastical governance, about those who were unwilling to accept the oversight of women.

of jurisdictions and an additional and organised body of conservatives outside the jurisdiction of the local hierarchy, and partly because some Catholic commentators have little sympathy with their theological and ecclesiological position.

So as always we work to resist the spread of denomin-ationalism. Pope Benedict, supporting the Archbishop of Canterbury's efforts to keep the Anglican communion together, has given short shrift to attempts to draw some in breaking up *koinonia* within Anglicanism.

That last paragraph proved to be a touch ironic, given what was to come in 2010. In the meantime, however, one must presume that Brooke Lunn had resigned because, as these contrasting quotations demonstrate, there was a divergence between his view of the future role of the Catholic League ('united not absorbed') and that of the other members of the Executive ('the old paradigm of reunion … has come to an end'). 'Following the Director's retirement', said a note in the January 2010 *Newsletter*, 'it was not possible for the other officers on the Executive to provide very much in the way of service during 2009 … we therefore felt it was only fair not to ask for members' subscription fees' – but they were now going to do so. It was indeed true that little 'in the way of service' to the membership had been provided. There had been no edition of *The Messenger* in 2008, and though there was an intention to produce one in July 2009, this did not happen. Nor was there, during 2009, any issue of the *Newsletter*. When it returned, in January 2010, it had a very different story to tell. It was headed '*Anglicanorum Coetibus* "It is accomplished: our Founding Principle"'.

Pope Benedict XVI's Apostolic Constitution of that name was dated 4 November 2009, the memorial of St Charles Borromeo. It begins:

In recent times the Holy Spirit has moved groups of Angli-cans to petition repeatedly and insistently to be received into full Catholic communion individually as well as corpor-ately. The Apostolic See has responded favourably to such petitions. Indeed, the successor of Peter, mandated by the Lord Jesus to guarantee the unity of the episcopate and to preside over and safeguard the universal communion of all the Churches, could not fail to make available the means necessary to bring this holy desire to realization.

It does not specifically make mention of which groups of Anglicans had repeatedly petitioned, and there was a strong suspicion both at Lambeth and in the Executive that they were from the 1991-formed Traditional Anglican Communion. Though these thoughts had been voiced in Committee, they were not mentioned in Mark Woodruff's enthusiastic response to the document, which appeared in the January *Newsletter*, an enthusiasm only moderately constrained by the recognition that 'Perhaps it is not the entire reconciliation of the Anglican Communion and the Roman Catholic Church that was in people's minds.'

What was envisaged by the Apostolic Constitution was the establishment of 'Personal Ordinariates', or quasi-dioceses, which would encompass some of the elements of the Anglican tradition, not least the ordination to the presbyterate of married men, though this, too, was somewhat constrained. It seems Rome did not consider this a permanent 'derogation' from the law of celibacy and, as is the discipline in the Eastern-rite Churches, there were to be no married bishops. The much-debated question of what constituted the Anglican patrimony, however, is at last given concrete form:

Without excluding liturgical celebrations according to the Roman Rite, the Ordinariate has the faculty to celebrate the Holy Eucharist and the other Sacraments, the Liturgy of the Hours and other liturgical celebrations according to the liturgical books proper to the Anglican tradition, which have been approved by the Holy See, so as to maintain the liturgical, spiritual and pastoral traditions of the Anglican Communion within the Catholic Church, as a precious gift nourishing the faith of the members of the Ordinariate and as a treasure to be shared.

Yet as Bishop Christopher Hill pointed out in *The Messenger of the Catholic League* for April–August 2010, 'the vast majority of any potential Anglican clerical aspirants [in England and Wales] have been using the Roman Breviary and significant parts, if not the whole, of the Roman Missal for many years'.[19] And many of the 'clerical aspirants' were celibate. To some it might therefore have seemed *plus ça change*, only with added papacy.

The papers published in this very substantial issue of *The Messenger* came from a variety of sources, and not all contributors saw things in quite the same way. Professor Eamon Duffy's article, for instance, would not have been at all to the liking of Fynes Clinton and others who held firmly to the belief that the Church of England was a direct descendant of the Pre-Reformation Catholic Church in England, the *Ecclesia Anglicana*.[20]

It is of course one thing to propose the establishment of Ordinariates. Quite another to bring this about. It was quite evident that the English and Welsh Roman Catholic bishops, despite protestations to the contrary, were not exactly enthusiastic about setting up a new form of jurisdiction within the Bishops' Conference. RC theologians, as Fr Woodruff reported after attending a conference on the Apostolic Constitution, were even less so. 'There had been some expressions of anger and disgust and concern at the action of the Holy See', he said.[21] The main thing, however, was to make the provisions work, and the Catholic League pledged itself to this task. One crucial aspect of the enterprise was finance, because the Ordinariates were expected to be self-funding. The Forward in

---

19 *Anglicans and Catholics in Communion: Patrimony, Unity and Mission* (London: The Catholic League, 2010), p. 106. This was a special issue of *The Messenger* containing a number of papers on the theme of 'patrimony, unity, mission'. It was edited by Mark Woodruff. Bishop Hill was Chairman of the Church of England's Council for Christian Unity.

20 It should perhaps be said that this, long ago, was also the conclusion of – the impeccably Anglican – Professor Z. N. Brooke in his *The English Church and the Papacy*, first published by Cambridge University Press in 1931.

21 Executive Minutes, 11 December 2009.

Faith movement had been receiving donations to support the new initiative, but as its own members were so divided they decided instead to ask the League to act as a temporary treasurer, and this was agreed.[22] A Blessed John Henry Newman Fund was set up to handle donations.

The establishment of the Fund was agreed at an extraordinary Annual General Meeting held on 30 October 2010 at the church of Christ the King in Gordon Square, London. The main purpose of the gathering was to endorse, which was duly done, the policy agreed by the Executive for the future of the Catholic League:

(i) We continue to see the Catholic League as a group for orthodox Anglicans and Roman Catholics focussed on the same faith as set out in the *Catechism of the Catholic Church*.

(ii) We will provide support, fellowship and guidance in the current period of discernment for Anglican Christians considering their position.

(iii) We agree that the League will assist the establishment and development of an Ordinariate in England.[23]

The Executive heard that the Ordinariate was expected to come into being early in the new year. An event, or several events, intended to inform Roman Catholics about the new structure within their Church were proposed by the League, but in the end did not take place. Nonetheless the League went ahead and helped to fund 'The Portal', a web-based magazine of information about the Ordinariate. At more or less the same time it sent a substantial donation for the work of the Anglican Centre in Rome.

As had been predicted, the Personal Ordinariate of Our Lady of Walsingham was set up on 15 January 2011. After the promulgation of *Anglicanorum Coetibus*, three Anglican bishops announced their resignation from their office as from

---

22 Executive Minutes, 24 August 2010.
23 *Newsletter*, September 2010.

31 December 2010 – resignations the Archbishop of Canterbury accepted with regret. With three nuns from the convent in Walsingham and a few others, they were received into the Roman Communion on the following day. On 13 January, the former Anglican bishops were ordained Roman Catholic deacons, and two days later Roman Catholic priests. One of them, Keith Newton, former Bishop of Richborough, became the Ordinary of the Ordinariate, with the title of Monsignor as a Protonotary Apostolic, and given the right to wear episcopal regalia together with membership of the RC Bishops' Conference of England and Wales.[24] Ordination to the office apart, Mgr Newton is a bishop as far as the membership of the Ordinariate is concerned – having married bishops being judged to be contrary to tradition. The establishment of the Ordinariate and the ordination of its first clergy were followed at Easter 2011 by the adherence of some 900 laity and 60 clergy. Most of those who were fast-tracked to RC priesthood had been priests with long experience of running parishes, something which the clergy of the Traditional Anglican Communion did not have.[25] The League added a prayer for the Ordinariate to its Apostleship of Prayer intentions.

Fr Woodruff's words, 'It is accomplished', quoted above,[26] might perhaps have marked the culmination of the Catholic League's mission.[27] *Anglicanorum Coetibus*, he said in a lengthy statement to the 2013 Annual General Meeting, held

---

24 All three were given the title of Monsignor, with similar rights to those of Fr Newton.

25 Membership is restricted to former Anglicans or to those 'lapsed' Roman Catholics brought back to the practice of their faith through the ministrations of the Ordinariate. At the time of writing (December 2015), there are just under 100 clergy in the Ordinariate, including a small number of deacons. There appears to be no public information on the number of lay members. In the USA, some members of the Traditional Anglican Communion had separated from mainstream Anglicanism as parish groups, and therefore their clergy, unlike those in Britain, had continued to have parochial responsibilities.

26 See p. 121.

27 The Executive had indeed been considering winding up the League before the publication of *Anglicanorum Coetibus*.

on 2 July in the Ordinariate church of the Assumption and St Gregory, Warwick Street, in London's Soho, was 'a tangible fulfilment of its founding witness to corporate reunion'. But its work was not yet over. Many of the League's 450 or so members remained devout adherents to the Church of England, while still eager 'to help it rediscover its essential unity with the Catholic Church in fullness of communion with Peter'.

The Annual General Meeting at Warwick Street in London took place exactly 100 years to the day from the foundation meeting at St Mark's, Bush Hill Park, Enfield. The centenary had not passed unnoticed. The League was believed to have been the first organization to lead a pilgrimage to the restored Marian shrine at Walsingham, and in 2013 there had been a centenary pilgrimage when Mass was celebrated for the souls of the League's founders. On 6 July there was a centenary Mass in Fyne Clinton's church of St Magnus the Martyr at London Bridge, for many years the centre of the League's activities: it was from there that Walsingham pilgrimages had set out. The following day there was another centenary Mass, this time at Corringham, where the Bishop of Richborough preached.[28] As more permanent memorials to the work of the League, a large monstrance, bearing the League's emblem, was given to the Roman Catholic church of Corpus Christi, Maiden Lane, which had been declared by Cardinal Manning a national centre of devotion to the Blessed Sacrament, and a plaque was to be placed in the League's chapel at Walsingham. And a history had been commissioned.

These actions appeared to be the actions of an organization about to dissolve itself. That, indeed, had been the tenor of some of the discussions in the Executive Committee in the immediate aftermath of the Apostolic Constitution, and 2013 seemed an appropriate time, after a century of activity bringing the Church of England closer to Rome, to close the League down. This has not happened, though there has been some very careful, and carefully documented, disposal of the League's assets. There are still pilgrimages, particularly those to Walsingham

---

28 *The Messenger*, Centenary Edition, August–October 2013.

and the ever-popular one to Bruges. There remain members, as the Priest Director remarked above, worshipping as members of the C of E but still hoping for unity with Rome, despite the obstacles placed by the ordination of women.

And there were still substantial funds. The League had been holding money for the Ordinariate, and this was passed on, together with £65,000, paid over two years to help finance its start-up costs. There were regular grants to a number of organizations and individuals, including to the Anglican Centre in Rome to allow students from the developing world to study for the priesthood close to the centre of Roman Catholicism.

The League continues to support Anglican–Roman Catholic dialogue, especially in the guise of ARCIC III, while fostering a wider ecumenism including the 'Reformed, Evangelical and other Protestant Church traditions', as it says on the website.[29] But its main focus is still where it began as Langford James and Fynes Clinton envisaged the Catholic League, specifically with the Church of England. And again, as it says on the same website,

> the League is supporting efforts to enable [those] who treasure and seek to conserve their historic religious and cultural patrimony in fullness of communion with the Catholic Church and the See of Peter to be able to do so, in a way that both leads to its greater development and to closer ecumenical bonds between the Catholic Church and the Anglican Church.

---

29 http://www.unitas.org.uk [accessed 17 December 2015].

Appendix 1

From + Cowderoy to Fr Willebrands

What follows is the text of a letter from Bishop Cyril Cowderoy, Bishop of Southwark (the diocese became an Archdiocese in 1965 and Cowderoy was elevated to the rank of Archbishop), to Johannes Willebrands, dated 23 February 1957. Willebrands, born in 1909 and ordained priest in 1934, had in 1952 founded in his native Holland The Catholic Conference on Ecumenical Questions, which had met annually in various locations. Apparently, he was eager to bring the meeting to Britain – his philosophical doctorate was on the thought of John Henry Newman – and out of courtesy asked permission of the local ordinary. In 1960 Willebrands was the first person chosen by Pope John XXIII as secretary of the Secretariat for Promoting Christian Unity, and in 1969 became the President of what was now the Pontifical Council for Promoting Christian Unity, shortly afterwards being named a cardinal. In 1975 he became Archbishop of Utrecht, a post from which he resigned in 1983. He died in 2006. The letter is in the Archives J. Willebrands at the Monastery of Chevetogne, and I am grateful to Fr Mark Woodruff for bringing it to my attention. It is dated from a nursing home in Ramsgate, and the underlining is as in the original text:

Dear Dr. Willebrands

Thank you for your letter of February 22nd.

I do not feel justified in giving any <u>approval</u> or <u>recommendation</u> such as you describe. At the most I would <u>tolerate</u> the presence of the delegation at the Conference, but I do not agree with it and I do not like it.

If these non-catholics desire to know what the Catholic Church teaches and what its views are on the points you mention, there are plenty of Catholic Bishops and Clergy in England to whom they can address their enquiries. The idea that Continental theologians will be more 'broadminded', 'more tolerant' and 'more understanding of the "Catholic" party in the Church of England' is ridiculous and impertinent.

Much harm has been done by meddlesome activities of Catholics from abroad who without any real understanding of the problem have formed contact with English heretics which only serve to confirm them in their opinions.

Naturally if the Holy See were to tell me that it desired this Conference to take place with Catholic representation, I would accept this at once. If the Holy See leaves it to me to judge, I would say No.

God bless you.

Yours very devotedly,

+ Cyril

Appendix 2

1932 Constitution of the Catholic League

THE CATHOLIC LEAGUE

CONSTITUTION

from

The Manual
PUBLISHED BY THE CATHOLIC LEAGUE
11 CITY ROAD, LONDON E.C.1
1932

DEDICATED TO THE MOST BLESSED TRINITY
UNDER THE PATRONAGE OF
OUR LADY OF VICTORY, SAINT JOSEPH AND
SAINT NICHOLAS
ON THE FEAST OF THE VISITATION B.M.V.
1913

IN NECESSARIIS UNITAS
INDUBIIS LIBERTAS
IN OMNIBUS CARITAS

THE OBJECTS OF THE LEAGUE

1. The promotion of fellowship among Catholics, and the Reunion of Christendom.
2. Conversion to the Catholic Religion.
3. The Sanctification of our Members.

THE BADGE

The Badge is a Key and Crozier, crossed in a small square. The key symbolizes the Church's authority and discipline in Canon Law and Penance; the Crozier, her pastoral work in Teaching and Sacraments. The Square is the Holy Church, the City which lieth foursqare and is at unity in itself, and a reminder of Christian perfection. The cord, on which the Badge is worn at services and meetings, is of blue for Our Lady and gold for St Joseph.

PATRONS

The League and its work were solemnly dedicated to Almighty God at its foundation in 1913, under the patronage of Blessed Mary, Our Lady of Victory, a title closely connected with the triumph of the true Faith and with re-union; and under the invocation also of Saint Joseph, Patron of the Universal Church, so beloved in the West; with Saint Nicholas of Myra, the wonder-worker, to whom devotion is especially given by Eastern Catholics. We have also in these Saints, patrons respectively of our women members, our men and our children.

FEASTS

The Anniversary is observed in May or June.

Members are asked to observe the following Feasts:

The Feast of the Most Sacred Heart
Our Lady of Victory, October 7th
The Patronage of Saint Joseph, Wednesday following the
Second Sunday after Easter
Saint Nicholas, December 6th
Each Chapter and Ward should also keep the Feast of its
Title, and its Annual Requiem.
The First Friday of each month is observed by the Apostle-
ship as devoted to the Sacred Heart, and all C.L. Priests are
asked to celebrate on this day on behalf of the League and
its objects.
An Annual Requiem Mass is celebrated each November on
behalf of all departed members.

ORGANIZATION

The League is organized territorially where possible in Chapters
(usually diocesan), which may be sub-divided into Wards. Over
each is a Priest and a Secretary. Close Wards may be formed
in connection with Homes and Institutions. Each member is
enrolled in the Ward or Chapter in which he is domiciled. He
may also be an *Associate* of another Chapter or Ward. Parish
and other Guilds may also be aggregated to the League, with
their members as C.L. Associates, under the same conditions of
membership as Postulants.

GOVERNMENT

The League is governed by the General Committee consisting
of the Priest-Directors, the General Secretary and officers, rep-
resentatives of the Sodality and League Priests, and of other
Sections, and elected members. Each Chapter by its Provost,
Ward by its Warden, Secretary and, when possible, by elected
Committee.

MEMBERSHIP

All the faithful, of whatever rite or country, are welcome as members, providing that they conform to the following conditions:

POSTULANCY

A year's postulancy (except for the Clergy) is required, on entering which a declaration is signed that the postulant (conformably with his age)

1. Is an instructed and practising Catholic and recognizes the duty of conforming to the discipline of the Church *especially* in the following points:
   (a) Attendance at Mass on days of obligation;
   (b) Confession at least once a year, according to the Paschal precept;
   (c) Observance of the days of Fasting and Abstinence;
   (d) The Fast before Holy Communion.

Note that the principle of Catholic discipline requires those who need relaxation (if not exempt) to see or avail themselves of dispensation from proper ecclesiastical authority.

2. Is desirous of promoting the objects of the League.
During the year care should be taken to deepen knowledge of the Faith and study 'The League's Profession of Faith', the Tridentine Creed.

FULL MEMBERSHIP

At the end of the year the postulant is responsible for applying to the Secretary for a form of application for full membership, in which he declares that he fulfils the above conditions and accepts as a standard of belief 'The Creed of the Council of Trent'.

The League has adopted this as being the simplest available document summarizing the Faith of the Western Church and of the Church of England before she was coerced by the state at the Reformation.

After election the member will be Received and Blessed by a Priest and invested with the Badge.

N.B. An Annual Subscription of at least 1/6 is required of all members and postulants. Subscription for Life-membership is 15/-.

Children remain as postulants until 16 years of age, paying 6d. Subscription. The Badge is the property of the League and must be restored on cessation of membership, when the deposit of 6d. will be returned.

CONSTITUENT SECTIONS OF THE LEAGUE

SODALITAS PRETIOSISSIMI SANGUINIS D.N.J.C.

THE SODALITY OF THE MOST PRECIOUS BLOOD OF
OUR LORD JESUS CHRIST

*Founded under the Patronage of St Charles Borromeo,
February 17th, 1914.*

The Sodality is founded to unite Priests under the obligation of Celibacy, and of the recitation of the Divine Office, in order that by mutual prayer and association they may cultivate in themselves and in the Church the highest ideals of priestly life, and of pastoral, ministerial and doctrinal proficiency.

The Sodality is dedicated to The Most Precious Blood in devotion to the Priestly ideals of Penance and Sacrifice, both in life and ministry.

THE OBJECTS OF THE SODALITY

(a) To promote the highest ideal of the priestly life in holiness, discipline and proficiency.

(b) To promote the objects of the Catholic League, *viz.*, the extension of the Catholic religion, Catholic unity and the deepening of the spiritual life of its members.

CONDITIONS OF MEMBERSHIP

The applicant for enrolment as Member or Associate shall sign:
(a) An undertaking to observe the Rules and to endeavour to promote the Objects.
(b) A declaration that he recognizes the duty of conforming to the discipline of the Church.
(c) A solemn affirmation that he recognizes that the reception of the Sacrament of Holy Orders constitutes a diriment impediment to Holy Matrimony, and therefore he acknowledges himself to be under obligation, in virtue of his Ordination, to remain celibate.
(d) An acknowledgement of the obligation *sub gravi* of the recitation of the Divine Office of the Latin Breviary.
(e) A declaration that he professes and holds the Faith as set forth in the Tridentine Creed.

RULES

(a) To offer the Intention at Terce daily for the members and objects of the Sodality.
(b) To make the Morning Offering of the C.L. Apostleship of Prayer.
(c) To celebrate Holy Mass with Intention for the Sodality and the League and their objects once a month; if possible on the first Friday; and, that day being free, a votive Mass, if convenient, of the Most Sacred Heart.
(d) To make an Annual Retreat of at least three whole days.
(e) To offer Holy Mass for the repose of the soul of a Member on hearing of his death.

Members and Associates of the Sodality, by virtue of their observance of Rules (a) and (b) are as such Members of Associates of the C.L. Apostleship of Prayer; and so are linked up with those who are united in this devotion to the Sacred Heart for the extension of Christ's Kingdom.

RECOMMENDATIONS

(a) To make, alone or with others, a monthly Retreat.
(b) To conform in ceremonial, as far as possible, with care and exactness to the Roman regulations.
(c) To submit a rule of life to a director.
(d) To continue the systematic study of dogmatic, moral and ascetic theology.

THE APOSTLESHIP OF PRAYER

The League has founded the Apostleship of Prayer on the model of the association of the same title in the Roman Communion.

THE METHOD

The *Rule of Devotion* consists essentially in making each morning an act of consecration of the life, work, sufferings and prayers of the day in union with the Most Sacred Heart of Jesus, and for all the intentions for which Our Lord makes ceaseless intercession in Heaven and offers Himself in the Holy Sacrifice for us.

The Rule of the First Degree

To undertake:
(a) To make daily the *Morning Offering of Consecration* of our prayers and life to the Sacred Heart, the following being the usual form:

O Lord Jesus Christ, through the most pure heart of Mary, I offer Thee the prayers, work and sufferings of this day, for all the Intentions of Thy Divine Heart in the Holy Mass, especially for ....

(b) To offer daily prayer for the League and its Objects, using either the League Prayer or Our Father and Hail Mary (or, as members of the Sodality and others, the Office of Terce for the same intention);

N.B. By the above words 'and its objects' is signified any one of its objects.

Those who are able are asked to extend this consecration further by undertaking one or both of the two remaining Degrees, which carry into further practice the principles of the Morning Offering.

The Rule of the Second Degree

To undertake to recite daily one Decade of the Holy Rosary. This may be fulfilled by following:

(a) The rule of the C.L. Rosary Confraternity, or
(b) The rule of the Catholic League Living Rosary of Our Lady of Victory for Catholic Reunion, or
(c) The rule of the Living Rosary of Our Lady and St Dominic, or other Rosary Society with daily recitation, or
(d) A private rule.

The Rule of the Third Degree

To undertake, by arrangement with the Director or one appointed by him, to make the *Communion of Reparation* on a fixed day once a week or at least once a month, after making Sacramental Confession within the week, with the intention of offering:

(1) Consolation and Reparation to the Sacred Heart for the outrage, unbelief and indifference to which the Blessed Sacrament is exposed in our Churches.

(2) Intercession for the increase of faith in and worship of the Blessed Sacrament.

There will be a natural desire to give alms for enriching the outward dignity of the Cult of the Most Holy Sacrament, as provided for by the Tabernacle Treasury.

Where possible members of the Third Degree should be grouped into bands of 7 of those who undertake to make this Reparation once a week, and of 30 of those who do so once a month, in order that the Communion of Reparation may be made daily and perpetually.

CONSTITUTION

The C.L. Apostleship is organized under a Priest-Director.

At the *Apostleship Altar* is kept the *Roll* of members to be continually brought before God in intercession.

As need arises, Local Promoters will be appointed to further the purpose of the Apostleship.

Particular requests for Prayer for Special Needs may be sent in by members to the Secretary of the Apostleship or to a Promoter, and these intercessions will be offered at Mass and recommended to members for intercession.

MEMBERSHIP

All members of the League are asked, if they are able, to join the Apostleship, and so give their aid to the work of the League and the advancement of God's kingdom.

To become a member, it is only necessary to sign and send in the form of undertaking to observe at least the Rule in the First Degree.

The Scapular of the Sacred Heart has been adopted by our C.L. Apostleship as a reminder of the daily Consecration and as our Livery of service of the Sacred Heart. It is a white Scapular, with an image of the Sacred Heart, and, on the other piece, of the Mother of Mercy. It is blessed by the Director with the proper form. It is worn over the shoulders of those who desire to receive it.

When members are enrolled at a meeting in Church, it is well that they should be publicly invested with the Scapular. Where this is not possible, it will be sent to the applicant after enrolment.

There is no annual subscription, but a *donation of 6d.* is asked for on being enrolled.

It is understood that if a member intends to cease observing the Rule, he will ask for his name to be removed from the Roll, as no longer fulfilling his share of what he seeks from others.

Departed members are transferred to a Roll of 'Expectantes', and they will have a continual share in the intercessions of the Apostleship, and will, we hope, continue to pray for us who are still militant on earth. Members should leave instruction that intimation of death be sent to the Secretary.

In special circumstances, persons who are not members of the League, may be enrolled as Associates, and share in all the spiritual privileges of the Apostleship.

RECOMMENDED AND ASSOCIATED DEVOTIONS

– To dedicate not only the Friday after the Octave of Corpus Christi to the Sacred Heart, but also the *First Friday of each month*.
– To receive Holy Communion or to attend Mass, if possible, on this day on behalf of the League and its several objects.
– *Priest-members* to say Mass, if possible of the Sacred Heart, for the same intentions, on the First Friday, or at least once a month; and (unless members of the Sodality of which this is a Rule) to send their names as contributing this help of their charity to the spiritual treasury of the Apostleship.
– To spend an hour in prayer in Church or elsewhere, between Thursday afternoon and sunrise on Friday, in memory of the Agony of Our Blessed Lord, especially in preparation for the First Friday Communion.

- To pray the *Prayer to the Agonizing Heart* of Jesus for the dying.
- Those in association as *The Cloister of the Sacred Heart* (or the *Guard of Honour*) to consecrate, without necessarily leaving their ordinary employment, a fixed hour each day to spiritual retirement and interior silence, in union with the Adoration of the Sacred Heart in the Blessed Sacrament; with attention directed toward a particular Tabernacle.
- To hear a second Mass on Sundays and days of obligation in place of those absent, to atone for sinners, and in reparation for the neglect of Divine worship.
- To pray the Holy Rosary in association with the Rosary Confraternity or as a member of a circlet of the Living Crown of Our Lady of Victory.
- To observe the Church Unity Octave.

THE ROSARY CONFRATERNITY OF THE SACRED HEARTS OF JESUS AND MARY

OBJECTS

The promotion and honour of the Most Sacred Heart of Our Blessed Lord; and of Our Lady.

To encourage among our members, and so spread abroad, greater fervency in the use of the Holy Rosary.

Intercession for the members and intention of the C.L. Apostleship of Prayer.

To promote solemnity and beauty in public worship and especially our League Processions. Members of the Confraternity may wear the processional Mantle of blue in honour of Our Lady, with a collar of red in honour of the Sacred Heart.

RULE

We invite members to be enrolled in the Rosary Confraternity, dedicated to the Sacred Hearts of Jesus and Mary, and to adopt as their rule – which is that of the ancient Dominican Con-fraternity of the Rosary – the recitation of the Fifteen Mysteries during each week; one decade in each five being recited in inter-cession for our objects.

Members should also use the Rosary in the way of meditation and endeavour to extend the knowledge and practice of it among others.

All members of the Confraternity are also members of the Apostleship by virtue of the *first rule* being that of the Apostle-ship 'Morning Offering', so that in this way the Confraternity is spiritually united with the other devotional Sections of the League.

(1) To observe the Rule of the First Degree of the Apostleship of Prayer, *viz.*, to make daily the 'Morning Offering'.

(2) To recite weekly the Fifteen Mysteries of the Holy Rosary of Our Lady.

(3) To say *one* of the Mysteries of each chaplet for the inten-tions of the Apostleship, or any *one* of these.

(4) To assist in Processions of the Blessed Sacrament and of Our Lady as far as possible in Confraternity Mantle, etc., when permitted by the Confraternity authority and requested by the promoter of the Procession. In the case of a member ceasing permanently to observe the Rule, the Mantle will be used, and should be given to the Confraternity.

(5) To wear regularly under the outer garment, the C.L. Apostleship Scapular of the Sacred Heart and Our Lady of Mercy, as a reminder of service and devotion.

THE LIVING CROWN OF OUR LADY OF VICTORY

The whole Rosary is offered as a Crown of Honour to Our Lady by groups or circlets of 15 persons who undertake to say one Mystery each day for the Intention of Catholic Reunion. The Mystery is changed monthly as assigned against the member's number in the 'C.L.Messenger'.

THE TABERNACLE TREASURY

A fund, dependent on donations, makes grants for maintaining the outward dignity of the Cult of the Blessed Sacrament.

THE CATHOLIC LEAGUE CHANTRY TRUST

This Trust has been established for the celebration of REQUIEM MASSES in perpetuity or otherwise for departed members and others.

It is administered by Trustees, members of the General Committee, who are responsible for the Masses being offered each year.

The first Chantry Mass so endowed is that for C.L. members who laid down their lives in the Great War.

A donation or bequest of £20 secures an Annual Mass in perpetuity, and single Masses will be celebrated for the accustomed stipend.

RETREAT ASSOCIATION

As a chief means of promoting our third object, yearly retreats are arranged for Priests and lay people. The Sodality holds a monthly Retreat for Priests.

PILGRIMAGE ASSOCIATION

Pilgrimages are regularly arranged to the National Shrine of Our Lady at Walsingham, and, as opportunity arises, to other sacred places at home and abroad.

REUNION

In pursuance of its first Object, the League initiated the *English Council for the Church Union Octave*, which now promotes its observance in co-operation with the League.

THE CHURCH UNITY OCTAVE

From the *Feast of St Peter's Chair at Rome,* January 18th, to the *Feast of the Conversion of St Paul,* the Apostle of the Nations.

It is only by the reunion of all Christians into the one Visible Kingdom of Christ, symbolized by the Chair of St Peter, the central See of Christendom at Rome, that the power of the Church can be directed, without the present waste and rivalry, to the conversion of the whole world by the One Faith in Christ our King.

Prayer, to be recited daily.

On the last day of the Octave, Holy Communion, after Confession, and a visit to a Church to offer a prayer for:

(a) The progress of the Faith and Triumph of the Church.

(b) Concord among Christian Rulers.

(c) Conversion of sinners.

(d) Uprooting of Heresies (*plenary indulgence*).

DAILY INTENTIONS SUGGESTED

Jan. 18 *St Peter's Chair at Rome.* The return of all the 'Other Sheep' to the 'One Fold'.

Jan. 19 Reunion of the Eastern and Western Churches.

Jan. 20 The repairing of the 16th century breach between England and Rome.

Jan. 21 The return of Lutheran and other European Protestants to Holy Church.

Jan. 22 The return of all Dissidents to Holy Church.

Jan. 23 The return to the Holy Sacraments of lapsed Catholics.

Jan. 24 The conversion of the Jews.

Jan. 25 *The Conversion of St Paul.* The Missionary conquest of the whole world for Christ the King.

RECOMMENDATIONS

1. Receive Holy Communion as often as possible during the Octave.
2. Attend Mass daily for the Intentions of the Octave.
3. Say a Decade of the Holy Rosary each day for the above Intentions.
4. Offer a penance, a fast, the Stations of the Cross, or some devotion as an act of Reparation for the sins of Heresy and Schism.
5. Offer Prayer or Intention at Mass every Thursday for 'Reunion with the Apostolic See'.
6. Study the question of Reunion, particularly as it affects these two Provinces [of Canterbury and York].

THE PRAYER OF THE LEAGUE

O Lord Jesus Christ, Good Shepherd of Thy flock, Who dost send Thy Church into all the world to teach the Truth and to gather all men unto Thyself; we humbly beseech Thee to send the blessing and guidance of Thy Holy Spirit upon us Thy Children who are united for Thy service in the Catholic League, that in all our words, our work and example we may set forward Thy Glory and the good of Thy Church. Grant by the intercessions of Thy Mother, the All-Holy and Glorious Ever-Virgin Mary, and of Thy blessed Saint Joseph and Saint Nicholas, our Patrons, that the hearts of our people may be converted unto Thyself and to Thy Holy Church, and that there may be strengthened in us the desire to accomplish Thy Holy Will for the oneness of Thy Fold. Inflame us with the fire of Thy Sacred Heart and grant to us a deeper faith and love; increase in us zeal for truth and service, and fill us, O Lord, with the spirit of penitence and godly fear: Who livest and reignest, One God, world without end.

OR

Almighty God, Who hast given unto us Thine Only-begotten Son Jesus Christ, to be the Way, the Truth and the Life, we beseech Thee to send Thy blessing upon all members of the Catholic League. Inflame us with the love of the most Sacred Heart, and deepen in us faith and penitence and zeal for Thy service. By the prayers of the Blessed Virgin Mary, and of Saint Joseph and Saint Nicholas, our Patrons, grant peace and unity to Thy holy Church: convert the hearts of all our people to Thy Truth, and guide and prosper all the counsels and undertakings of the League to the glory of Thy Name and the maintenance and advancement of Thy holy religions: Who livest and reignest One God, for ever and ever. Amen.

PRAYER OF THE APOSTLESHIP

O Lord Jesus Christ, Who hast promised that wheresoever two or three are gathered together in Thy Name Thou wilt be there in the midst of them: look down with compassion and love upon us who are now united before Thee in lowliness of heart to honour Thy Most Sacred Heart, and in the desire to make It known and loved by all. Come into the midst of us and fill our hearts with Thy blessings and inflame them with the fire of Thy love, Who livest and reignest God for ever and ever.

Appendix 3

The Constitution of the Catholic League

as amended at the Annual General Meeting on 3 March 2008

Name and Objects

1. The League shall be known as the Catholic League.
2. The objects of the League shall be:
   a) The promotion of fellowship among Catholics.
   b) The union of all Christians with the Apostolic See of Rome.
   c) The spread of the Catholic Faith.
   d) The deepening of the Spiritual life.

Membership

3. The League shall consist of Ordinary Members, being people who assent to and practice the Catholic Faith as defined by all the Councils of the Church, up to and including the Second Vatican Council and post-conciliar documents. The League recognizes the *Catechism of the Catholic Church* as an authoritative guide to this rich deposit of Faith. All members must pay the annual subscription in accordance with rule 11.
4. Any person desirous of being admitted to the League as a Member must normally be proposed by a priest; a priest-member of the League must normally propose applications received from a priest. Elections shall take place by majority of members of the Executive present at a meeting of the Executive of the League. The form provided in the Manual shall admit members.

5. A member may be removed from the League by resolution of three quarters of the members of the Executive present at any Executive meeting. Any member so removed has the right of appeal to the Annual or a Special General Meeting of the League.

6. A member shall be deemed to have resigned from the League when his subscription is two years in arrears. Such a member may revive his membership without re-election upon payment of his arrears of subscription. The Executive may waive the requirement for repayment of arrears.

7. No member whose subscription is in arrears shall be entitled to vote at any meeting of the League.

8. Members shall have the privilege of wearing the League's badge, which can be purchased from the Secretary at a cost determined by the Executive.

9. Members have the privilege of a Memento at Mass on notification of death and thereafter annually.

Sodality of the Precious Blood

10. This is an autonomous constituent section of the League for priest members who accept the obligation of celibacy and of the recitation of the Divine Office. Further details are in the first part of the Manual of the League.

Subscriptions

11. The annual subscription for ordinary members shall be determined by resolution of the Executive, subject to endorsement by a majority of the members present at an Annual General Meeting.

Meetings

12. Ordinary General Meetings shall be held at such times and places as the Executive shall determine. Such meetings, including local chapters, are primarily designed for the

furtherance of the League's objective as set out in Rule 2. Executive business may be transacted at these meetings but shall be kept to a minimum.

13. An Annual General Meeting shall be held within each calendar year. The purpose of the Annual General Meeting shall be to receive the report of the Executive, to pass the accounts, to approve the elections of such members of the Executive and Officers as may be necessary and to transact other business as may be required and it may be competent to do. Notice of the Annual General Meeting, together with the agenda and the accounts, shall be given to members not less than fourteen days in advance.

14. A Special General Meeting may be summoned at any time by the Executive, who shall be bound to do so on receipt in writing of a request, signed by not less than five members, stating the business to be transacted. Not less than fourteen days' notice shall be given to members.

15. The quorum for the transaction of business at an Annual or Special General Meeting shall be ten members and at other meetings, five members, including at least one officer as defined in rule 26.

16. The voting at all meetings shall be by majority vote and shall be by a show of hands unless a ballot be demanded by at least one quarter of the members present.

17. Members shall have the privilege of introducing guests at Ordinary Meetings.

Publications

18. Publications of the League shall be made available to members either free of charge, or on such terms as the Executive shall determine.

Retreats and Pilgrimages

19. The Executive shall organise retreats and pilgrimages in furtherance of the League's objects set forth in Rule 2.

20. Members shall have the privilege of introducing guests on retreats and pilgrimages.

Governance

21. The management of the League shall be vested in an Executive, consisting of the Officers of the League who shall be elected at the Annual General Meeting and any members co-opted to serve on the Executive in accordance with the provisions of this Rule. Members of the Executive who are absent for more than two consecutive Executive meetings, without good reason, shall be deemed to have retired. The Executive shall have the power to co-opt up to three members where necessary, who may include a representative of the Sodality of the Precious Blood and the Priest Director of the Apostleship of Prayer, to serve for terms of no more than four years at a time, but who may be eligible for further co-option if necessary. The 'Executive' fulfils the function and responsibilities of both 'Managing Trustees' and 'Holding Trustees'.

22. Any five members may nominate for election as an Officer of the League any member not currently, or continuing to serve as, a member of the Executive, in writing signed by them and delivered to the Secretary one week before the Annual General Meeting, the date of which shall be published in *The Messenger* or *The Newsletter*. No member may sign more than one nomination for any one election. Each such nomination to be valid must be accompanied by a written agreement from the candidate so nominated to the Secretary expressing willingness to serve on the Executive. Duly nominated Officers shall be elected members of the Executive at the Annual General Meeting by a majority of those present and voting and shall retire in rotation after a period of not more than four years, being eligible for re-election thereafter. The order of rotation of retirement shall be determined at the first meeting of the Executive after this constitutional provision takes effect.

23. At a meeting of the Executive three members including one officer shall constitute a quorum.

24. Any reasonable expenses incurred by members of the Executive in fulfilment of their work will be reimbursed by the League.

Minutes

25. The Executive shall cause proper minutes to be made of the proceedings of all meetings of the League, of the Executive and of any committees of the Executive and all business transacted at such meetings and any minutes of any meeting if signed by the chairman of such a meeting or by the chairman of the next succeeding meeting shall be conclusive evidence of the facts stated there in.

Officers

26. There shall be up to six Officers of the League who shall be the Priest Director (who shall normally be the chairman), the Secretary, the Treasurer, the Membership Secretary, the External Relations secretary and where necessary an additional secretary. The Officers shall be appointed by an Annual General Meeting of the members of the League by a majority of those present at the meeting and shall serve for not more than four years unless removed by the Executive by a majority of those present at the meeting. Officers shall be eligible for re-election. In the event of a casual vacancy in an office, the Priest Director may appoint someone to carry out the duties of Office until the next Annual General Meeting. In the event of a casual vacancy in the office of Priest Director, the Executive may elect one of its members as the new Priest Director until the end of four years from the last Annual General Meeting at which a Priest Director was elected. A Vice-Chairman, who may be a priest or layperson, shall be elected annually from amongst the Executive members to serve for one year.

Property and Assets

27. (a) The property of the League, other than cash which shall
be controlled by the Treasurer, shall be vested in the
Executive. The Executive shall deal with the League's
property and any reasonable expenses incurred by them
in the fulfilment of their trust shall be reimbursed by the
League.

(b) The Executive shall be entitled to employ a bank, trust
corporation, or other appropriate professional body to
hold the League's investments and other assets in its
name as nominee for the League and may delegate to
such organisations the power to vary investments and
other assets from time to time. The terms of such delegation and the scale of charges therefore shall be in the
hands of the Executive to decide.

(c) The Executive shall have power to invest the League's
funds in the purchase of or at interest upon the security
of such stocks shares securities or other investments
(including land or any tenure) of whatsoever nature or
wheresoever as they shall in their absolute discretion
think fit to the intent that they shall have the same full
and unrestricted powers of investing and transposing
investments in all respects as if they were an absolute
beneficial owner.

(d) The Executive shall have power to direct the Treasurer
to exercise some or all of its responsibilities in respect
of the League's property and assets and in accordance
with its direction and not otherwise. The Treasurer
shall report on the exercise of these responsibilities at
the meetings of the Executive and the Executive shall
review the financial position of the League with the
Treasurer at least annually.

The President

28. The President of the League shall be elected, by the Executive, for life. The President shall have been a member of the League for at least ten years and have served at least one term of office on the Executive. The President may be removed from office by resolution of the Executive by a majority of those present at an Executive meeting. Together with the Executive, the President shall have a responsibility to maintain the good standing of the League and to fulfil the specific duties in rules 31, 32 & 33.

The Accounts & Auditors

29. Once a year at least the accounts shall be examined and the correctness of the income and expenditure accounts and the balance sheet ascertained by one or more qualified auditor or auditors or independent examiner appointed by the League in Annual General Meeting.

Committees

30. The Executive may delegate any of its power to committees consisting of members of the Executive and co-opted members and any committee so appointed shall conform to any regulation imposed on it by the Executive.

Dissolution of the League

31. The League may be dissolved on the recommendation of the President, the Priest Director and the Executive and by resolution of the members at two Special General Meetings summoned for that purpose, the second of which shall be held not less than twenty one days after the first.

32. On dissolution of the League all its property shall be dealt with, as the members by resolution at the second of the two meetings shall determine provided that the proceeds of the

dissolution shall be given to a charitable body with similar aims and objects.

Alteration and Interpretation of Rules

33. None of the rules may be altered or rescinded or new ones added except by resolution carried by three quarters of Members present at a General Meeting of the League, special notice having been given previously to all members of the proposed alteration. In the event of any dispute or doubt arising about the interpretation of these Rules, the Executive shall seek the opinion of the President and his decision shall be final.

DAILY PRAYER OF THE CATHOLIC LEAGUE

Almighty God, You gave us Your only Son, Jesus Christ to be the Way, the Truth, and the Life; we ask You to send Your blessing upon all members of the Catholic League. Inflame us with the love of the Sacred Heart and deepen in us faith and penitence and zeal for Your service. By the prayers of the holy Virgin Mary, our patron, grant peace and unity to your Church. Convert the hearts of all Your people to Your truth and guide and prosper all we do in the League to the glory of Your Name and the extension of Your Kingdom. We ask this through Christ our Lord. Amen.

DAILY PRAYER FOR CHURCH UNITY

Lord Jesus Christ, Who said to Your Apostles, Peace I leave you, my peace I give you: look not on our sins, but on the faith of Your Church, and graciously grant her peace and unity in accordance with Your will; Who live and reign for ever and ever.

DAILY PRAYER IN HONOUR OF MARY MOTHER OF THE CHURCH, PRINCIPAL PATRON

Father of mercies, Your only Son, hanging on the Cross, gave us His Virgin Mother Mary to be our Mother also. Under her loving care may her children grow daily in holiness, so that all humanity may see in Your Church the mother of all nations. We ask this through our Lord Jesus Christ, Your Son, who lives and reigns with You and the Holy Spirit, one God, for ever and ever. Amen.

THE MORNING OFFERING OF THE APOSTLESHIP OF PRAYER

My God and heavenly Father
I offer you the Precious Blood of Jesus Christ
and all that I shall do or suffer this day
in union with him. And I pray
> *Sunday* – for the Holy Father Pope Benedict and the needs of the Universal Church
> *Monday* – for the sick, housebound and people with disabilities
> *Tuesday* – for the Catholic League and its work for the Unity of Christians
> *Wednesday* – for the Church's witness to peace and justice
> *Thursday* – for my bishop, my Church community and our greater growth into Christian unity; and for the unity of all Christians with the Apostolic See of Peter at Rome
> *Friday* – for forgiveness for the sins of separation and the conversion and unity of all humanity in the truth and love of Christ
> *Saturday* – for a deeper love of our Lady, Mother of the Church, among Christians and for the ecumenical work of the Shrines at Walsingham, Egmanton and Ipswich. For the souls of the departed.

Notes on the 2008 Constitution

By the 1980s, the structure of diocesan wards and local chapters no longer existed.

Sodality of the Precious Blood

The Sodality for priest-members of the League who have made a promise of celibacy and to celebrate the Liturgy of the Hours in accordance with the rite of the Latin Catholic Church, remains a constituent association of the League, although it effectively became an organization in its own right.

The Apostleship of Prayer

All members of the League are automatically members of the Apostleship. They are requested to make the Morning Offering, to observe the First Friday devotion to the Sacred Heart in reparation for the sin of Christian disunity and dishonour to the Eucharist and the worship of God, to pray and offer intention for the League's objects (which had been re-defined and expanded), and to pray each Thursday for the visible unity of Christians. The regular *Newsletter* issued by its Priest-Director promotes particular intentions, as well as carries news about the League's work.

Confraternity of the Rosary

The Confraternity of the Rosary and the Living Crown no longer exist, but members are encouraged to pray the Rosary as part of a personal rule of life with intention for the League's objects. Many members of the League continue its focus on promoting devotion and pilgrimage to the Blessed Virgin Mary through active membership of other associations, which the League supports spiritually and materially. These include the Society of Mary, the Ecumenical Friends of Fatima, the Ecumenical Marian Pilgrimage Trust, and the two pilgrimage organizations based in Walsingham: the (Roman Catholic)

Walsingham Association and the (Anglican) Society of Our Lady of Walsingham, in the foundation of which the League's own founders were instrumental.

Tabernacle Treasury

Work in promotion of the worthy celebration of and devotion to the Eucharist among Anglicans is no longer undertaken by the League, being for the most part pursued by the Confraternity of the Blessed Sacrament. Its last works were to gift all remaining vessels and vestments to the parishes which had enjoyed them on loan, to give a complete set of liturgical vestments to the restored Martyrs' Chapel at the Dowry House run by the Community of Our Lady of Walsingham, which is open to pilgrims and retreatants of all Churches, and to donate a monstrance for the restored national Shrine of the Blessed Sacrament at Corpus Christi, Maiden Lane.

The Catholic League Chantry Trust

The Apostleship's Priest-Director, an Anglican priest, maintains the Roll of Departed members, and offers the celebration of the Eucharist for the repose of their souls. Members are notified of those who have died and asked to pray for the repose of their souls. In 2017 the League paid for the complete refurbishment of the Chantry Chapel associated with the League and the Sodality of the Precious Blood at the Anglican Shrine of Our Lady of Walsingham.

Retreat Association

An annual retreat is provided for priests by the Sodality of the Precious Blood.

Pilgrimage Association

The League conducts an annual pilgrimage to the Precious Blood and Our Lady of the Vine in Bruges. Each shrine has long been associated with prayer for Christian unity. From 2003 the League among other organizations has been a sponsor of the Ecumenical Marian Pilgrimage Trust, whose biennial pilgrimages to Walsingham for Orthodox, Catholic, Anglican and Free Church clergy and faithful now take forward the League's foundational promotion of pilgrimage to Our Lady of Walsingham in hope of the reunion of Christians in the one Church of Christ.

English Council for the Church Union Octave

The Apostleship of Prayer annually issues devotional and liturgical resources for the observance of the Week of Prayer for Christian Unity on the lines promoted in England and across the world by Fr Paul Couturier in the 1930s, based on the Church Unity Octave founded in 1908 by the Catholic Franciscan Friar of the Atonement in the United States, Fr Paul Wattson SA, and Fr Spencer Jones, the Anglican vicar of Moreton-in-Marsh and an early member of the League. Since the Second Vatican Council, the annual Week of Prayer has become an official collaboration between the World Council of Churches and the Vatican's Pontifical Council for Promoting Christian Unity. Since this is locally served by Churches Together in Britain and Ireland, there has been no need for a distinct voluntary association to promote the Week of Prayer. The Apostleship's resources complement those from official sources.

Bibliography

Beauduin, Lambert, *L'Église Anglicane unie non absorbée*, Malines, 1977.

Church Times online edition.

Cuming, G. J., *A History of the Anglican Liturgy*, 2nd edition, London: Macmillan, 1982.

Curtis, Geoffrey, *Paul Couturier and Unity in Christ*, London: SCM, 1964.

Dick, John, *The Malines Conversations Revisited*, Leuven: Leuven University Press, 1989.

Doolan, Brian, *The First Fifty Years*, Crux Press for the Catholic League, 1966 [?].

Farmer, Robert, *The Catholic League 1913–1988*, The Catholic League, 1989 [?].

Hebblethwaite, Peter, *Paul VI: The First Modern Pope*, London: Harper-Collins, 1993.

Hostler, Ethel M., *Charlotte Boyd: Some Notes on Her Life*, The Catholic League, 1996.

In This Sign Conquer: A History of the Society of the Holy Cross (Societas Sanctae Crucis) 1855–2005, London: Bloomsbury, 2007.

Keble, John, *Keble's Assize Sermon: Centenary Edition*, London: A. R. Mowbray, 1931.

Knox, Ronald, *A Spiritual Aeneid*, 2nd edition, London: Burns and Oates, 1950.

Maiden, John, *National Religion and the Prayer Book Controversy*, Woodbridge: Boydell & Brewer, 2009.

The Messenger of the Catholic League.

Norman, E. R., *Church and Society in England 1770–1970*, Oxford: Clarendon Press, 1976.

Oxford Dictionary of National Biography online edition.

Palmer, Bernard, *Gadfly for God*, London: Hodder and Stoughton, 1991.

Pickering, W. S. F., *Anglo-Catholicism: A Study in Ambiguity*, London: Routledge, 1989.

Salter, John, *The Anglican Papalist*, London: Anglo-Catholic History Society, 2012.

Smith, Charles, *A Pocket Guide to Walsingham*, London: Mowbray, 1988.

The Tablet online edition.

Tricker, Roy, *Mr Wason ... I Think*, Leominster: Gracewing, 1994.

Walsh, Michael, 'The Conservative Reaction', in Adrian Hastings (ed.), *Modern Catholicism: Vatican II and After*, London: SPCK, 1991, pp. 283–88.

Walsh, Michael, 'Ecumenism in Wartime Britain', *Heythrop Journal* 23 (1982), pp. 234–58, 377–94.

Walsh, Michael, *From Sword to Ploughshare*, London: CIIR, 1980.

Walsh, Michael, *The Secret World of Opus Dei*, London: Grafton Books, 1989.

Ward, A. Marcus, *The Pilgrim Church*, London: the Epworth Press, 1953.

Woodgate, Michael, *Foxes Have Holes*, The Catholic League, 2005.

Woodruff, Mark (ed.), *Anglicans and Catholics in Communion: Patrimony, Unity and Mission*, London: The Catholic League, 2010.

Yelton, Michael, *Anglican Papalism: An Illustrated History 1900–1960*, London: Canterbury Press, 2008.

Index